Foreboding

Poems

1992 to 2024

YELLOW TIGER PRESS

Geoff Beacon

geoffbeacon@yahoo.co.uk

COPYRIGHT © 2024

Geoff Beacon

All rights are reserved. No part of this book may be reproduced, distributed, or transmitted in any form or by any means, including photocopying, recording, or other electronic or mechanical methods, without the prior written permission of the author, except in the case of brief quotations embodied in critical reviews and certain other non-commercial uses permitted by copyright law. For permission requests, write to the author at the address provided in the acknowledgements section of this book.

Thanks to NASA and @Unsplash for the Earth Image

Printed By:

Book Printing UK

First Printing Edition, 2024

ISBN: 978-1-3999-9877-2

Contents

Table of Contents

Sycamores..11
Russian Roulette..12
Sonnet 18a - Unfinished......................................13
Reluctant revenge...14
Manifesto...15
The Leopard..16
NOSIC - King of Property Rights.........................17
Playing with fire in Gillingham Park....................19
Returning from Ruskin..20
National Curriculum Biology, Lesson 9..............21
Mockbeggar Farm...22
Sleeping Beauty Makes a Bonfire.......................23
Memo to the National Council 24
for Vocational Qualifications..............................24
He never went north of Watford........................26
Well Wouldn't You?..27
Memo to the lawyer: 28
The Coming of the Millennium...........................29
The Education Debate..30
Christian Values..31
An ending in three acts......................................32

In memory of the Iraqi who stayed at No 44......34
Green Activist in grams CO_2 per km [*]............35
Swimming In The Dark..36
Mary's Geography Lesson.....................................37
Roulette..38
Frankie And Johnnie Weren't Lovers..................39
The Open University, Programme 5....................40
Ladies and Gentlemen..42
Have a Banana I Dreamt......................................43
Fuck it Fuck it Fuck it..44
Reunion..45
Send Me Your Poor, Send Me Your Hungry........46
Does She Shave Her Legs?..................................48
Resuscitation..49
One Performance Only..50
Selling to the Emperor 51
Ladies and Gentlemen - a PENTAMETER...........52
Academic facts...53
Family values, England.......................................54
After a hard week, a Semantic Shift in Whitby...55
An Unfortunate Gift...56
Only the English...58
Current Rate of Exchange:..................................59
The lucky ones..60
Sex in the sea...61
More selling to the Emperor...............................62
Was Gordon Brown joking ?................................63
SEX IN SPACE...64
Then the king answered and said 65
The Phillips Curve..66

The Phone Call	67
Madonna Nudes 1979	68
Leaving the ERM	72
Adolf Grunbaum	73
Remembering Paris	74
Not meeting an English poet	76
Headmasters	78
Did I really write this??	81
Inarticulation	82
A tenner's worth more to me than the Queen	83
Come friendly bombs don't fall on Slough	84
Give me land lots of land	85
Billy Butlin's song	86
The Cantor Wankers Club [*]	88
If I'm in God's image - he'll be like me	89
At the Ordnance Survey	93
Sunstroke on Ilkley Moor, LS29 2BT	95
Learning by Rote	96
Driving home for Christmas	98
A Sentence	100
The Universe is Holonomic	101
How to draw a curve with one flat point	103
Park and Ride	104
Nostradamus, the FT and a Pareto Optimum	106
Rosetti's Wombat	107
"Old soldiers never die they only fade away"	109
Christine	110
Firelady	111
Family values USA	112
You're never alone with a Strand	113

An ambiguous cataphoric reference...............115
Condemn a little more......................................116
Superprofiles: The Affluent Achievers.............117
One for you, Brian...119
Reality - An Ostensive Definition.....................120
Sub-nuclear Naming..122
They still don't know what they did.................124
DECAL can map it...125
Let's Try..126
A New Mission Statement...............................128
The Real Thing..129
British Manufacturing Industry........................131
Set aside 133
Twenty years of madness thinking I know how 135
Chomsky...137
A Keller of a Joke..139
Memories of Paris II..140
Costs of the Psyche..142
The ghost of Albert Speer...............................143
Ordinal Utility..145
Spot the deliberate mistake............................147
It ain't the news today, O Boy.........................148
Kincora Boys Home...149
Why labour subsidies cannot work..................150
Plymouth, England, the World........................151
Difficult Times...154
News of the Symptoms...................................155
Oranges and Lemons......................................157
Kent or Mexico?..158
Uri...160

Superprofiles lifestyle E.................................161
Travelling by train..162
The boat-train from Tramore..........................163
Californians (Life Value : $1.5m)....................164
Film Quiz...166
Every Body Tells a Story................................168
The Convert...169
Exam question 6: 171
Lessons in Politics No. 3................................172
Green shoots at Canary Wharf......................173
Da-di-dadi-Daaaa-da....................................174
Remembrance...175
Millennium Bridge (2092)..............................176
Billy Butlin..178
A losing streak..179
A pleasant sensation.....................................180
The Empirical Test...181
Please forgive much of this...........................183
Redressin the Balance...................................184
High Energy Physics or..................................185
Happy End..186
After Birth..187
Middle Age Stress...188
Sinning...190
An Infinite Coastline in a Transient World........191
You are my Freudian slip...............................192
Smug-Oxbridge Bastard.................................193
Architects, the semantics..............................194
Back in the 1960s...195
Repeal the Safety Act....................................196

How it is..197
Idiots...198
Body Shape and Sporting Success...................199
God's (self) Indulgence................................201
Death of Lennon..202
Julie Andrews...203
The answer to unemployment, ...204
"Everybody knows somebody 205
killed in a car crash"..................................205
Memo to the linguistics department...............207
Twenty nine, Twenty nine............................208
It's too late now..210
Crossing to the other side............................211
Memo to the Principal.................................213
Liverpool lullaby.......................................214
Tate Gallery to Portobello Road is 6 miles........215
Housing Bingo..216
West Side Story..217
Time has lost its meaning............................218
Parmenides..219
Philosophers - the essence..........................221
Heigh Ho, says Roly...................................224
There's always a way to earn a living..............225
Lump of labour...226
A fading photograph..................................228
The Boat Show...229
One way bulimia.......................................230
Messages on the Millennium Bridge...............231
About time too...232
He was born in York - but didn't stay..............233

MacNeice pastiche	235
There's no place like home	236
Another Tempest	238
Take it from the Kop	241
BBC discovers global warming	243
Flagellation for poets	245
Trying to be Brave	246
Change of syllabus	248
One performance only	250
A call from a daughter (1998)	251
Not my cup of tea	252
Betrayed	254
Back from the hills	256
Help !	258
Crop Circles	259
Rickshaw Ride II	261
Mouthing through the windows	262
Range Rover Chant	263
Lady Lays	264
Poetic Parasites	265
Maps of thoughtful love	266
The silence	267
Night worker at Drax - An Obituary	268
He knew his place	270
Humans	271
At the Co-op Party Christmas dinner	272
One Ice Cream	274
Net zero 2030	278
OK Paul. One for you	280
Annie	281

Epilogue..282
Geoff Beacon remembers:................................282
Extra: Links to old websites.............................286
Note on finding references in the text 287

Sycamores

Outside my window
Little sycamore saplings
Grow in peace
Through the cracks in the path

For legal reasons
I must destroy
Their delicate green lives

For now they are defenceless
But their time may come
When we and our cruelty
Are gone

I hope so - don't you?

Russian Roulette

At the top the roller coaster slows its pace
Waiting for the certain downward rush
Just as the weighted chamber almost stops
But fortunately hardly ever does

The bullet in the gun must know its place
And mostly keeps its gamblers alive
We pray that God has given us this grace
As drunks we drive our world around the skies

Sonnet 18a - Unfinished

Shall I compare thee to an autumn evening
Drifting through the mists of time
Oft' times your lingering memory forming
Another inspiration for a rhyme

So calm your present state of irritation
Accept with Joy a well-meant sideways wink
Your distant ripples found in these creations
Will give you life much longer than you think

Auntie Jayne (2024) writes:

> That's quite a clever pastiche, Geoffrey. I'm not trying to humiliate you but just consider the final lines of the original:
>
> "So long as men can breathe or eyes can see,
> So long lives this, and this gives life to thee."
>
> It puts you in your place, doesn't it?

Reluctant revenge

So I pushed your young son under the bus
Shh. Don't make a fuss, don't make a fuss
You made the mine that killed fourteen of us
Call it quits your young son under the bus

I grieve for your son under that bus
He seemed such a nice boy, like the youngest of mine
Who went to the fields and was killed by your mine
Who went to the fields and was killed by your mine

With his mother, his brother, his sister, his aunt
I try to forgive but I know that I can't
My life is over, my life is gone
You've others to live for so you must live on

The wounds in my side are still oozing with puss
From the bits of the mine you made to kill us
Your whole lovely family'd be under that bus
If we did to you what you did to us

If we did to you what you did to us

Manifesto

I'm now a poet
But not very fine
At prosodic structure
Or elegant rhyme

My dream is just to even the score

It's not the elegance
But the violence

I do it for.

The Leopard

Be gentle with the leopard
Who cannot change her spots
She's got a serious purpose
That other cats do not

The compulsive hunting instinct
Is rooted in her past
It was long ago and far away
Her defining die was cast

She lies in wait for hours
And sometimes even years
Her inscrutable appearance
Allays her victims' fears

She captures their attention
With a powerful allure
They stretch themselves with pleasure
Silent and secure

Be gentle with our leopard
Even as she prowls to kill
For there's few of us who wouldn't
Join her in her thrill

NOSIC - King of Property Rights

(Blaydon Races - but spoken)

> They shan't violate my property rights
> They shall not take my taxes
> They shan't invade my peace and quiet
> They mustn't make a noise at night
> They must keep clean or out of sight
> As my wealth it waxes.

(Rocking chair)

> If they want to survive
> They can do it without
> Invading my privacy
> Threatening my property
>
> They must make their living
> As best as they can
> To help out their lot
> I needn't be giving

(Statement)

Its none of my business how they find their happiness

(Train on the track)

> They have the right
> And I had it too
> To make something of themselves
> Like you did too

(Blaydon Races - but spoken)

    The underclasses must
    Find their own salvation
    Feather-bedding indolence
    Weakens our great nation

    They must find a form of trade
    To afford their daily bread
    If it is they can't do that
    They can starve until they're dead

(After Nosic)

    Perhaps the upper classes could
    Fuck the underclasses daughters
    Then the underclasses could
    Have some income like they ought to

With appropriate enforcement of valid contracts

(Number taking with a New Right Tory Student,
A nice lad actually

"So no taxes at all?" --"That's right?"

"What about paying the Police?"

"No Police. Private guards for private property."

"What happens when there is a fight in a public place?"

"Public places. We aren't going to have those."

Playing with fire in Gillingham Park

The crowds at the fireman's wedding saw
The apprentices at the top of the
Not-yet-burning paraffin-soaked stage-set
Waiting for a well-timed spectacular rescue

Lillian's mother Lillian let out
That stage-set's painful scenes
Only once or twice in her lifetime

Lillian's daughter Lillian
Suppresses them still
Memory firmly locked in liquid nitrogen
To prevent vapourisation

***

Windscale (UK) Ltd will crash
Engine 46009 into concrete buffers
Cell Mutation Corporation will demonstrate
Their new range of benign marker viruses

***

The firework display has been postponed
But the bonfire will warm six billion onlookers
The finale will show rescue services in action
When a stage-set as big as the world is set alight

Returning from Ruskin

*Smell affects a primitive part of
the brain warns Jonathan Miller*

The smell that affected the primitive brain
Made his slumbering consciousness sit-up and start
The hormone release rocked him back in his seat
Raising echoes of memories from times that had passed

The smell that affected his primitive brain
Made his arms encircle a ghost from the past
An involuntary reflex sure and secure
Grasped the air as her shadow escaped from his grasp

The smell that affected his primitive brain
Made him know in a leap where his brother had been
Her fragrance had followed him onto the train
As unease and desire and regret mixed again

The smell that affected his primitive brain
He scrubbed clean with the force of the visual present
With the jokes he had told to the girl on the tube
As they got off and laughed at Mornington Crescent

National Curriculum Biology, Lesson 9

Strategies for genetic advantage

Now I've seen it on the telly
So I'm sure it's really true
For survival of the fittest
She goes for that illicit screw

She times orgasmic motions
To suck her lover's juices up
But with you, her best meal ticket
She comes too soon - you're out of luck

So you've got her where you want her
And she's shouting out with joy
You're proud to make her happy
But she's playing with you, boy

His superior genes inside her
Warm and bursting into life
But she loves you as she cuddles you
And would like to be a faithful wife

The sadness in this story
Is mistaking God's fine game
He's made these complications
To tease us with our macho pain

Jesus loves the little bastards
In your heart you know it's true
So when you pay their ballet fees
He'll smile and grin and think of you

Mockbeggar Farm

My father told me
At Mockbeggar Farm
The Lord of the Manor
Kept himself warm

By a fire, by the window
He sat down to eat
So beggars could see him
As they passed in the street

He laughed at their hunger
He laughed at their pain
He laughed and he laughed
Again and again

The trouble with seeing
Them starve on TV
Is that they can't see our comfort
They can't sense our glee

Sleeping Beauty Makes a Bonfire

The garden briars and buddleia trap our place of memories
Undisturbed for twenty years

Their branches, leaves and thorns preventing any footfall
Except the occasional cat

The sun lights up these misty images trapped in their cage
As they shimmer with the leaves

Until the noisy cruelty of the Black and Decker
Rips them up to disappear in garden smoke

Memo to the National Council for Vocational Qualifications

Train a hundred hair dressers to dress up our hair
And a hundred plumbers to fix up our taps
And a hundred bricklayers to lay all our bricks
And thousands of trainers to train them to fix
         My hair
         My taps
         My garden wall
I must have my hair cut three times more
Find leaky pipes I didn't find before
Have an extension put on my house
And have more children to fill them

But I'm not spending my money at all
I'm saving it up to spend on my soul
So what will we do with bricklayers and plumbers
That we have trained in enormous numbers

We'll take on some trainers to train them again
In flexible thought and assertiveness
And trades that will have future usefulness

But who will train trainers
train trainers trainers
train trainers trainers trainers

Whoever it is at the top of the tree
They must be clever, as clever as me

For we'll certainly see that in fifty year's time
We'll need lots of rhymers to make our rhymes rhyme

Now that we know, we've just got the time

To train trainers trainers trainers
Who will train trainers trainers
Who will train the trainers
Who will train us

In fifty year's time
I'll be starting the course
In elegant rhyme

But like the old lady
That swallowed the horse
I'll be dead of course

He never went north of Watford

And did those feet in Ancient Time
Never go beyond Highgate Hill?
Was it orphans in London Town
That lived in dark Satanic Mills?

But you wouldn't build Jerusalem
Anywhere near Berkley Square
The price of land is far too high
And people there will pass you by

But don't we need to start again
Having screwed our cities up?
Let us start near Princes Park
And build on down to Albert Dock

Lovely buildings bought with slaves
Can live again and show the world
The evil deeds of men now dead
Can be turned and used for good

Better people don't have cars [*]
Better people hate Milton Keynes
Better people want to live
Back in proper towns again

[*] The European Commission's study "Ville sans Voitures" showed that the same quality of life in "motor car" towns costs up to five times as much as in towns without cars.

Well Wouldn't You?

The join in the belt passed twice a minute
Hot and steamy heaps of green beans
Flowed in a stream that lasted all summer
The limp smug student scruffs kept at it
Picking out the warm wet slimy husks
With their white and wrinkled fingers

In the corner the army swimming team
Worked efficiently at their nice little number
Boxing up the cans
With the rhythm of a well-drilled team
Red berets folded under their epaulettes
They co-ordinated mechanically
Stopping sharply at break-time

"You should always marry a good-looking girl
Then you can put her on the game
And take life easy"

He listened with a trying-to-please smile

His own weak smile
Haunted him for days

Memo to the lawyer:

What's the copyright position
of the last two lines?

      I like Blake
      I like Donne
      I like your shout
      When you come

      But apart from a few
      Of them like that
      You can sod off
      With that poetry crap

      I just need
      This puerile shout
      To get this bile
      And anger out

      No masturbation of my emotion
      I'd rather do it with my cock
      "But it ain't the meat it's the motion
      That makes your momma want to rock"

The Coming of the Millennium

The Earth has magnetised your back
The Earth has magnetised my front
Your body squeezed between us both
The Earth impassive as I grunt

The Earth can feel a billion backs
Pressing on it every night
Is it still a well known fact
They'd all fit on the Isle of Wight?

The Education Debate

"Shakespeare's the only discipline they get."
(Anon: Today Programme, Radio 4, 1993)

> To be (Swish)
> Or not to be (Ooooh)
> That is (Swish)
> The question (Ooooh)
>
> Whether 'tis nobler on the behind to suffer
> The canes and slippers of outrageous spanking
>
> (Ring 0898 696969)
>
> Or to feel the discipline of rigid minds
> Who come to bury Shakespeare
>
> Not to praise him

Christian Values

I close my eye.
I shut my mouth.
I cannot hear
The madman's shout

We turf them out
From their warm old prisons
To become down and outs
To get soup from the missions.

I close my purse
I shut my eye
At the unhinged loonies
Who stink and die.

Praise God us High Church Christians have
Had the sense to stop
All this meek and mild
Love-your-neighbour crap.

An ending in three acts

God's commandments

Kill My world as little as you can
Don't drive in cars,
Don't fly in planes
And leave that corned beef in the can

Build on My world but do it with great care
Don't build with bricks
Don't build with steel
Don't build tall buildings in the air

Don't kill My world by rushing all the time
Gaze at My stars
Breathe in My air
Praise all creation which is Mine

Satan's temptation

We'll fly you over burning forests
We'll walk you through the starving hoards
We'll show you drowned and bloated corpses
At a price you CAN afford

You'll glide above the sky in comfort
You'll sleep your nights in quiet hotels
You'll sit and watch our views in wonder
Of people in a billion hells

God's judgement

You were the stuff My dreams were made of
You were the stuff My dreams were made of
You were the stuff My dreams were made of

Now your little world will be ended with My sleep

In memory of the Iraqi who stayed at No 44

At the match ...

>God, don't the rockets look beautiful.
>Woooosssshh, woooosssshh, woooosssshh.
>
>A triumph of British technology.
>
>From the steam engine, to the jet engine to the most beautiful killing machine in the world.

The score ...

>Arsenal 90,000 Baghdad 6.
>Bagdhad included guest players from New York Jets.

The celebrations ...

>We made MINCEMEAT of them.
>We are the champions.
>We are the champions.
>
>We made MINCEMEAT of them.
>I bet their mums had lots of trouble getting
>Their kit clean when they got home.
>
>We made MINCEMEAT of them.
>Shred finely with little bomblets.
>And leave to dry in the sun.
>Cover with sand for a thousand years.

Green Activist in grams CO2 per km [*]

Green Island
(Reached by Air) 684

Green Wellies
(After a drive in the car) 83

Green Landrover
(For travelling afar) 99

[*]New Scientist 11 July 1992. Reporting figures from ETSU, Harwell.
Figures are on a per seat basis.. Land Rover estimated as 1.2 cars.

Swimming In The Dark

I begin to dream of you again
You are swimming in the dark
You pull your legs together
You thrust your legs apart

You are wearing only bracelets
And droplets in your hair
I am swimming close behind you
And breathe your breathed out air

The water's warm about us both
The ripples hardly sound
I catch you up quite slowly
You do not turn around

My brain's becoming captured
For instinct likes this dark
The warm and soft and floating
From aeons in the past

We glide together slowly
We slow the speed of time
With rhythmic consummation
Our souls are intertwined

My body taken over
My mind is lost in space
But it's Wednesday morning's garbage men
Outside when I awake.

Mary's Geography Lesson

As she holds the whole world in her hands
Tormented spurts of blood and cries of pain
Remind her of her long-gone lover's plans
And sear her palms and fingers once again

Each explosion of a hidden mine
That rips the flesh and splinters childish limbs
Wells up the stores of sadness in her mind
For those that screamed and also those that did

Working at their manufacturing plants
She knows they know the harm they really do
She feels the slimes of guilty consciences
That soften up their regions of the world

As she holds the whole world in her hands
Deserted by her lover and his son
She feels relief the end is nearly nigh
And so at last her misery is done

Roulette

Since the summer of 1917
Frank's son Frank knew
Existence was more than mortal consciousness

From the of top Burham Downs he had seen
The fabric of the sky drop from its scaffolding
To show the reality beyond

Frank's father Frank never got the chance
To share his son's revelation
His dying body was returned from French
                                         battlefields
To a wife who said

There must be some mistake
This is an old man
My husband is young

Frankie And Johnnie Weren't Lovers

Johnnie was a romantic
He could feel the falling satellite as it sped
                            sighfully overhead
And as it fell it saw from high the Earth's
                            curvature dropping away
So it never reached its goal

Frankie was a trucker
Warm and cab-high above the road
She commanded all around her
As wheels on the ground she headed for Turin

Back at HQ, near junction 19, Johnny tracked her route

        She was driving through Champagne
        He was bathing her in Champagne

        She was climbing up the Alps
        He was showing her the heights

        She was passing through the Dolomites
        He was making a pass for her

        That was his 15th pass this week
        His 50th pass this month
        His 679th pass this year

        Her strong hands gripped her wheel
        Her whole body gripped his mind

        They would have made a lovely couple.

The Open University, Programme 5
Rural India - A Vulnerable Life

He stopped at the frame where she smiled for the camera

    The young mother in her pale sari
    Had that magnetism
    Found in the screen-tests of Hollywood myth

    Sitting in the hired rickshaw
    With three neat and well-behaved children
    Her husband smart in his Sunday-best

In the darkness he wound back the editing proof
To reverse the rickshaw silently past the waving bushes

    The whole family passed his screen test
    But made no other films

    Their crops had not done well
    The six silver birches they could not sell for firewood
    So her husband had rented out their plot of land

    He had not proved strong enough
    To earn much with his rickshaw

    So at the crossroads
    They paid the rickshaw's new owner
    And waited for the bus

> To take the children to grandparents
> And them to labour in the brickfields
> Where they would save up to buy a buffalo
> And try to sell the milk

Leaving the studio he went downstairs
Switching off the lights on every landing

In the noise and fumes of the Charing Cross Road
He caught a cab to his favourite vegan restaurant

Ladies and Gentlemen

For your delectation
And your pleasure.

For the spiritual journey
Of a lifetime....

We are bringing you tonight
The greatest English poetic mystic

William....

Blake

And his sidekick
The greatest spirit guide of them all....

The one and only....

Chief....

Sitting....

Bull

Have a Banana I Dreamt

As I floated down the Strand
People were stuck to the ground
Slowly writhing

The ghost of Christmas past
Popped out of the theatre
For a breath of fresh air

A ghost with shell-shock
Who would jump with fright
At the drop of a pencil

His lungs once burnt with poison gas
He had smelt the corpses
Rotting on the wire

He looked across the Strand
At the cold grubby bodies, which washed away

His memories of Marie Lloyd

And meeting boxer Jack Johnson,
              (hated in America)
Remembering him as a rather pleasant gentleman.

Then he slowly dimmed and vanished

He could not face another act
Of this comedy of errors

Fuck it Fuck it Fuck it

We'll die before it's over
We'll die before it's dead
It'll screw reincarnation
It'll dog our aeon's head

It's not something we desire
It's just stuck here in our heads
A forceful lingering presence
We'll die before it's dead

Reunion

Kevin accelerated past the corner shop
To blow the wind through his toes
A year later he returned to the squat
With the cigarettes he had been sent to buy

"Hello Kevin", they said, "did you remember the matches"

***

"My Frank is coming for me", said Kate an hour
before her death, as if the 50 years of uncompromising
survival were an eye-blink.

***

But yesterday

Without eye-contact
With the formalities of words at their least coherent
We could clearly see the preserved reality
Behind your own personal time-locked door

Send Me Your Poor, Send Me Your Hungry

(London, 1785)

He wandered through each dirty street
Near where the dirty Thames did flow
And saw in every face he'd meet
Marks of weakness, marks of woe

He saw so many children poor
The chimney sweeps among the snow
Loosely wrapped in clothes of death
And taught to sing their notes of woe

But westwards in America
He prophesied an Age of Gold
No longer lands of poverty
Free from hunger, free from cold

William Blake was a supporter of American Independence, seeing Americas a place to escape the poverty and cruelty of the old world. About the time he was writing his poems about the plight of London's poor, he helped save Tom Paine, author of 'The Rights of Man', from the gallows.

(Pittsburgh, 1885)

He wandered through each dirty street
By Monongahela's timeless flow
And saw in every face he'd meet
Marks of weakness, marks of woe

He saw so many children poor
The urchins begging in the snow
Loosely wrapped in clothes of death
Crying out their notes of woe

His people gone, his Tribelands taken
By the greedy search for gold
He gave what he had to foreign urchins
Starving in the Eastern cold

Just before the genocide of his people and the confiscation of Native American Lands, Chief Sitting Bull joined Buffalo Bill's Wild West Show for a season.

Annie Oakley remembered his shock at the poverty and squalor of the big Eastern cities: most of the money he earned, $50 a week and $1.50 for each signed picture, went into the pockets of small ragged boys.

Source:"The Wild West",
Channel Four Television, London.

Does She Shave Her Legs?

The naked angel floats to heaven
Rising up in heavenly thought
I glance and glance away quite quickly
In case my interest is caught

Her strong and muscular behind
The silky feel above her knee
Her body odour strange and different
For angels aren't like you or me

If I am good and go to heaven
If rectitude can rule my life
I think I'll be in heaven in heaven
With angel in the afterlife

Resuscitation

The boy on the postcard stood on his toes
In the summer sea at Reculver Sands
He could not swim but gulped his breaths
From the troughs of the waves passing overhead

The sun warmed muddy green light
Rocked him gently as he drifted deeper
And jumped to breathe

Later he remembered the crunch of the pebbles
As his foot slid slowly down the slope
With the grown-up thought that he was still too young
To have a much of a life to flash before him

One Performance Only

You work so hard to earn enough
To fly around the world

You work so hard to earn enough
To fly around the world

Reward yourself ...

    We'll fly you over burning forests
    We'll walk you through the starving hordes
    We'll show you drowned and bloated corpses
    At a price you CAN afford

    You'll glide above the sky in comfort
    You'll sleep your nights in quiet hotels
    You'll sit and watch our views in wonder
    Of people in a billion hells

You deserve it.

Selling to the Emperor

Look at this school-gown, the salesmen said
Only the wise see its scholarly thread

It will make your kids clever, learned and trained
They'll see with their eyes and think with their brains

Use this gown that is sewn with our secret thread
And your subjects shall prosper, the salesmen said

Jane, 20, working as researcher at the Radio Station, gave up the chance to improve her typing because the course director insisted Jane also took the NVQ module in photocopying.

Philip, 17, wants next year off. He thinks college is crap but he does quite like it when he has to act the part of a storeman once a week. But that is not a job he will ever do.

Roger, 42, manages highly specialised computer courses. He is sceptical of computer science graduates. He finds them rather short on deliverables but they can write weighty reports describing the simplest of tasks.

Timo, 23, is a history graduate. He has found it almost impossible to get work that uses his degree. But he is glad he has not sold out like many of his contemporaries and started accountancy training.. That would be a waste of his hard won knowledge.

Ladies and Gentlemen - a PENTAMETER

When lines like this can spread them smoothly out
The five soft beats can easily disappear
But in that tune that Brubeck carefully made
The rhythm in our minds blasts two then three

Academic facts

We let out our knowledge a fact at a time
In five-thousand word chunks and elaborate prose
You will understand if you go through the grind
How we keep up our funding so nobody knows

       What we're doing
       What we're paid for
       Because we hide it all
       Behind tortuous syntax
       And obscure verbal walls.

Family values, England

Mrs Dickens stood on tip toe

Out of the attic window she could see
Her son and daughter go to their music lesson
In the opposite house

For several years she had hoped that
Just one time they would turn round

And look up

And give her
        one
          small
        wave

She was, as Charles had told her, a bad mother

So, she stood on tip toe
Unable to call through her imaginary bars

After a hard week, a Semantic Shift in Whitby

Shagged (1)

Sleeping sleeping surfacing shagging sleeping
Swollen
Sleeping sleeping surfacing shagging sleeping
Slippery
Sleeping sleeping surfacing shagging sleeping
Sliding
Sleeping sleeping surfacing shagging sleeping
Sore
Sleeping sleeping surfacing shagging sleeping

Shagged (2)

An Unfortunate Gift

Looking down in the darkness we could see the explosions in
    India dock
I counted the seconds for the flash of the blast from the last
    bomb I dropped
The buzz of the biplane was left far below us as we cut the Earth
    free
We floated on Air as we followed the Thames right down to the
    sea

Then at dawn across Dogger we lifted the sky
Our steel and gas ship rose seamlessly free

    ***

Tuesday, September 5th, 1917, I burnt alive.

I could hear the faint cheers from Edinburgh Road, Luton
(A suburb of Chatham, Kent) drifting up from below.

    ***

Lillian's daughter Lillian was lifted over the fence
The others ran round the long way to get under cover.
It is still Lillian's daughter Lillian's first terrifying memory
The huge shape hanging quietly above them, dispensing death.

    ***

    But for Lillian's mother Lillian the fear
    Was lost in her tears
    She could see them
    Without seeing them

As the flames lit the sky
The crowd cheering
Lillian: Oh those poor boys

As the flames lit the sky
The crowd cheering
Lillian: Oh those poor boys

She could see them
Without seeing them
An unfortunate gift.

No conchie
A patriot
God WAS on her side,

But she could see them
Without seeing them -
An unfortunate gift.

Only the English

It makes me really proud
To be English

We all cheered when Tom Dooley scored
USA 1 England 0

Only the English can view their country
                            with such disdain.
That's something to be really proud of.

Current Rate of Exchange:

1 commission = 1000 omissions?

I'd like to teach them	Right from wrong.
I'd like to them to know	Their evil ways.
I'd like to hear	Their victims gloat.
I'd like to see them	Shut away.
I'd like them to feel	What it's like

    To be poor
    To be homeless
    To be ill
    To be hapless.

To be caught at the restaurant without a clean napkin.

The lucky ones

We subsidise their mortgages.
And pay for their degrees
But they're jumping every queue
Every time they sneeze.

They spread their grime with their big cars
Driving kids to school
But the scruffy and the unwashed
Must still abide their rules

The scruffy and the homeless
Must stay right out of sight
They should know what's wrong is wrong
And what's right is right.

Sex in the sea

Disappointment

> Take it from me
> Sex in the sea
> Isn't as nice
> As you'd think it'd be.

Ten million years later

> Take it from me
> Sex in the sea
> Isn't as nice
> As it used to be

Vaseline

> Take it from me
> Sex in the sea
> Can be almost as nice
> As it used to be

In the nineties

> Take it from me
> Sex in the sea
> Should always be done
> With the strongest condom

More selling to the Emperor

Look at this school gown the salesmen said
Only the wise see its intellectual thread

Hear the swish of the gown as it sweeps through the air
The grace of its lines will make the world stare

Manufactured in Germany, designed in France
To a Japanese style, you can see at a glance

It will make the kids clever, clever and bright
They all will have jobs, they'll be alright

When you clever people see the glint of the thread
Your kingdom will prosper, the salesmen said

OK Els,

>UCL have the best department for Beowulf
>>>>in the whole world

>My fried Derek used to tell me that Goole
>Had the only floating Tom Pudding hoist
>>>>also in the world

>Touché ?

>But you'll go on to great things. You essay on that
>pretentious poet was an inspiration.

>But for us old folks, do speak a little slower.

Was Gordon Brown joking ?

God please let Gordon Brown be only joking
About us having all the best jobs in the world
If we put everybody into higher education

I hope he says it just so he can win the next election

SEX IN SPACE

As we drift though outer space
In this weightless habitation,
You cannot sit upon my face
Without the pull of gravitation.

Then the king answered and said ...

Solomon had a hypothesis
That one harlot valued
The baby more.

He just didn't know
That inter-personal comparisons of utility
Were unscientific.

In retrospect isn't it amazing
That someone so ignorant
Could rule a kingdom.

The Phillips Curve

It's the same the 'ole world over
Ain't it all a blooming shame
Its the rich wot gets the pleasure
And the poor wot gets the blame

Its the rich wot cause inflation
And the poor wot's out of work
So sod you Mr Phillips (*)
You academic berk.

Its the rich wot spends the money
Its the poor wot feels the pain
So squeeze those overspending sods
And give the poor some jobs again.

(*) The Phillips curve embodies the well know fallacy that it is impossible to have low inflation and full employment.

The Phone Call

You had thrown the money down
And had said you said
"Damn him, Damn him he's not in."

He knew it was a double lie.
(One for her and one for him.)

But he thought you never would
Until you did.

Madonna Nudes 1979
or
(The Joy of Sex)

"They were nude studies, devoid of prurient interests, having nothing to do with sex or exploitation and that is just is how they should be viewed."
    Martin Hugo Maximilian Schreiber.

Martin Hugo Maximillian Schreiber
I'm sorry to let you down
Your joyous pictures of her pubic hair
Make my knees weak
Make my heart beat
Make my brain spin round and around.

As I'm consumed in fantasy's passion
I kiss the nape of her neck
I put my arm round her waist
And without undue haste
Feel her soft warming flesh
And controlling my eagerness
I'll pick her up, lie her down
On the rug on the ground.

I'll kiss her eyes
Kiss her lips
And stroke with my fingers
Her soft rounded tits
Tongue in mouth

Tongue in ear
Stopping to hear
Her breath breathing out

Under arm to smell her sent
Breathe in, breathe out
And holding her left arm bent
A tongue trace down her inside arm.
Another along her slender wrist
So the space between fingers
Are all gently kissed.

Back up the other arm
That's soft and smooth and glowing warm
My lips gently slide
Followed by a quick surprise
Of little nibbles down her side

She'll respond to me like I want her to do
I'll lick down her shapely leg
And suck softly every toe
I'll kiss her ankle
Her knee and her thigh
She'll gently respond
Respond with tremulous sigh.

And to give her more pleasure
I'll blow gently on
The sex between hips
Then I'll lick with my tongue
Through soft swollen lips
Till she's most modestly come.

Then my head in her thighs
I'll lie there and sigh
I'll feel with my lips
Those soft naughty bits
Slippery with passion.

I'll breathe slowly in
And get strength from the smell
That comes from the well
That focuses sensation.

I'll lay lightly on her
And make a slow penetration
So she will feel the pleasure
Of the entering sensation
Slowly at first
And then slowly faster
I'll rhythmically press
Till I get what I'm after.

A gentle moan, a soft shout,
A short grunt, a loud shout.

If my memory works well and I've not lost the knack
She'll lay on her side
I'll slip in from the back.
She'll put her hand over and grip on my balls
She'll turn her head round and give me a kiss
I'll wriggle and grind in heavenly bliss

Till I shout and I groan and I shudder with pleasure
Then we hold and we cuddle and reflect on each other

We will doze and doze ---in a comfortable way
                              with love in our hearts
With sweat, warmth and softness we'll sleep
                        through the day.
Sleep like the angels sleep, Sleep with our souls intact

Feeling that God's made us never to part.

Feeling God's smiles

Perhaps you could tell me Maximillian Schreiber
When your pictures evoke feelings like this
Are they prurient, crude, not born of your art
Or are you just another sexless old fart.

Leaving the ERM

Seven billion Euros lost sinking the pound
Seven billion Euros lost sinking the pound

That's seven billion loaves of bread.
And there's eight million to be fed.
Since one million's already dead.
That's one thousand loaves of bread. (*)

For each one left alive.
For each one left alive.

(*) Mother's Pride prices.
Hope they don't want fishes too.

Adolf Grunbaum

Adolf Grunbaum wrote a five-hundred word sentence.
Not understanding I put down the book.

Now I'm quite clever, one way or another.
(Particularly high on the old Watson-Glazier).
But if you've actually read it your better than me.

So Adolf Grunbaum's clever big book
Got him the tenure to write another.

I must try and get it and read it and count it.
To find if he has a new Guinness entry,

What mind, what intellect, what genius we see.

Remembering Paris
"Marylin Monroe se tuer"

Barry Riley (FT. 5th September 1992) :

Between 1m and 1.5m home buyers, mostly young, are technically insolvent with
"negative equity".A clash of the generations
is looming. The "woopies", the well-off older people who traded down in the housing
market in the late 1980s and banked the net
proceeds are enjoying a double payoff, with
an income bonus to add to their capital windfall.But no nation can expect to lure
its young into financial ruin and get away
with it.

> The peaches had smells.
> They never do here.
> The metro had smells.
> Like it doesn't do here.
> All Paris had smells
> Like it doesn't do here.
>
> I want to return. I want to return.
> But I've lost my chance.
> I should have got out when the clever ones did.
> Then I could spend my "Year in Provence".
>
> If I'd sold my house then.
> Like the clever ones did.
> I could buy Paris.
> Leaving mortgage to kids.

Suffer the little children.
They'll never pay their mortgage off.
They've lost out on their houses.
But at least they're not sleeping rough. [*]

Provence is nice
Provence is nice
Own your own home
With the roll of a dice.

When your number comes up
Flee to the sun
Flee to the smells
On unearned income.

[*] Except for children from the following target markets:

Superprofiles H23 - Unskilled Families, Inner City Conversions
Superprofiles I29 - Blue Collar Workers with High Unemployment
Superprofiles I30 - Low Income Older Families in Flats
Superprofiles I34 - Very Low Income Council Houses
Superprofiles J35 - Highly Unemployed in Crowded Council Houses
Superprofiles J36 - Large Unemployed Families in Cramped Council Flats.

Not meeting an English poet

(The Rumbling Tum, Liverpool, 1969)

> After we'd finished our fried egg butties.
> The Poet sat down while we spoke our FORTRAN
> (You know that Poet that makes love on a bus.)
>
> Now that was when I was still English.
> (Before the chips on my shoulder had set.)
> So
> We didn't see him.
> We didn't hear him.
> We refused recognition.
> In that English of ways.
>
> We kept speaking FORTRAN.
> We kept speaking FORTRAN.
> God, forgive us, forgive us,
> For being so boring.
>
> The silence we filled,
> To hide our confusion,
> With long FORTRAN statements,
> With more FORTRAN code.
> God, forgive us, forgive us,
> For being so boring.
>
> The noise of the silence of non-recognition,
> Was noise in my eardrums,
> Was noise in my eardrums.
> God, forgive us, forgive us,
> For being so boring.

It was soon after that I stopped being English
Now I'm sure that I could make love on a bus. (*)

(Poetry gig, York 1980)

Now I'm egocentric.
This may be imagined.
But after the Poet made love on his bus
He read one about OUR FORTRAN STATEMENTS
(I couldn't be sure, But it could have been us.)

I'm glad I'm not English.
I'm glad I'm not English.
I'm glad that I can make love on a bus.

But our English Poet
Who really is English.
I'd like to see him,
I'd like to hear him,
I'd bet that he wouldn't,
Make love on his bus.

I'd bet that he wouldn't,
Make love on his bus.

He had a DREEEAAM, He had a DREEEAAMM
He may not come there with us
But he saw the other side.
He may not come there with us
But he saw the other side.

Headmasters

Power corrupts.
And sends headmasters mad.

Teacher Dave had a head
That stood on the table
And directed school dinners
With a whistle and cane.

Teacher Gill had a head
Who spent all his time
Perfecting the photocopier
For the schools weekly newsletter.

Schoolboy Geoffrey was scared of the head.
Who used psychological warfare against the boys.

"Come in.
"Take your coat off.
"Hang it on the chair.

"Take your trousers down.
"Bend over.
"Why did you do that?"

"Because you told me to, Sir."

The warfare so successful
They didn't stop and think
There's something funny going on
This man is on the blink

But when the German master burst in,

All he said was

"Oh, sorry to interrupt, Sir."

The disapproving vibes of had their effect.

"You can pull your trousers up now."

But vibes are easily suppressed.
The warfare continued.

In later years, they called his bluff.
The times were changing to that hippy stuff.
He lost control but Geoff was glad to be gone.

The grudge wasn't deep enough
To want to feel the embarrassment
Of that strange man's bitter confusion.

Perhaps it's not just the power they have.

It's also the unaccountability.
Report to the governors once a month

Who have little accessibility.
Who cannot see the day-to-day.
Who aren't that bothered anyway.

If you don't like a neighbour
Then you can avoid them
If they're rude in the shop
You can shop elsewhere.

But that battle of wills
Between teacher and pupil
Has no resolution.
It lasts for years,
And years and years and years.

I just wish my will had been stronger.
That's what my pride tells me

But as every hooker knows
Its hard to win against the head.

Isn't it Sarah?

Sarah, I knew your headmistress as someone that ran a good school. In my list of heads, probably the best. I don't know the whole story but clearly she screwed up your life. She shouldn't have had that much power.

Did I really write this??

i see i see
i say i say
i do i do
don't you don't you

i close my eye
i shut my mouth
i cannot hear
the madman's shout

as we turf them out
from their warm old prisons
to become down and outs
to get soup from the missions

i close my purse
i shut my eye
at the unhinged loonies
stinking and dying

even if i had
an ambulance badge
my mouth to mouth
wouldn't bring them round

mouth to mouth
on yellowing teeth
taste their slime or
let them die in the street?

let them die in the street!

Inarticulation

I never seem to say it right
Confusion wakes me every night
Articulation gone it seems
So I must rhyme my mixed up dreams

When Axle's grandma said to him
Speak when your spoken to
Axel shut his mouth and grinned
So her caravan burned inside Berlin

A gipsy caravan burned away
A gipsy grandma had her say
A just reward for she that who
Says speak when you're spoken to

A tenner's worth more to me than the Queen

But I if I'd been to see Carnap, I wouldn't have misunderstood.

I would still have been able to say
    "A tenner's worth more to me
    than it is to the Queen"
and be able to avoid Bridgeman's fallacy.

    Lionel,
    What about the thicko's who
    Later on followed you.

I put it down to the bomb's charisma.

    Bomb power.
    Physics clever.
    Chemistry quite.
    Maths good.

So all the dim ones were left doing economics.[*]
And the ones that weren't dim had about as much creativity as accountants.

    Words the won't out
    Dam burst is about

    Dam burst is about
    World nought. World nowt

[*] OK, Peter. There were exceptions.

Come friendly bombs don't fall on Slough

Westfield's worse for humans now

Give me land lots of land

"Give me land lots of land
"And the sunny skies above
"Don't fence me in"

Don't ask me why
Don't ask me why
This song reminds me
Of the lonely screw fly

The screw fly that saw the man
Who was sleeping rough
The screw fly landed on his nose
And laid inside eggs enough

Eggs enough to kill the man
The man from Arkansaw
Who loved the open spaces
Who didn't like indoors

At first he thought he had a cold
Which wouldn't go away
But as the eggs hatched in his nose
They ate his brain away.

Note: Today we'd treat it with malathion

Billy Butlin's song

Now ...

    Let us accept refugees can't
    Drive their Land Rovers
    Or live in Provence

    But with modern technology
    I bet that I could

    Give them a home
    Where no buffaloes roam
    With all mod cons and also a phone

    Do you think that we should?

So ...

    That they could exist
    Drink wine and get pissed
    Enjoy what they'd missed

And where they could ...

Lead decent lives in four hundred square feet
At least while they're waiting to hear
If they can fly to America, England or France
But let's stop them invading our lives in Provence

Somewhere to live for a few hundred quid
Somewhere where bombs won't cut off their legs
Somewhere warm where the electrics not off
Somewhere to be where the kids don't all cough
Where the TB that killed my uncles is not
Where you walk to the shop without getting shot

Yet you middle classes sneer at my camps.

The Cantor Wankers Club [*]

They know what I mean.
They know who they are.

They get away with it because you're too ignorant to understand.

Isn't it just intellectual masturbation?
Inventing Algebras that never will have an interpretation?
Is it more useful than doing the Guardian Crossword?
How much do you get paid for doing it?
Has anybody every found an application for it?

You shouldn't ask me after a bottle of wine.
A friend of mine did get a job with a computer company.
Don't know what he did but it must have been useful.
Mustn't it?

How long have you been Head of Department?

(OK. The four colour theorem was quite interesting.
But wasn't its proof boring.)

[*] Georg Cantor, founder of a useless branch of mathematics.

If I'm in God's image - he'll be like me

Arthur shouts "Fuck you God"
Every time he drops a box.
It's fun to see old ladies jump
He only does it 'cos it shocks.

If I were God and a vengeful man
(For perhaps I'm in his image made.)
I'd laugh to see our Arthur shout
It's for believers I'd save my rage.

You pass on the other side
As other images of me die
Of hunger, torture, helplessness
And all you do is look and sigh.

For you believers on your daily ride
Around the M25.
As the fire that's coming next time
Whimpers from your car's behind.

You do it even though it's true
That drought and storm and pestilence
Follow in your daily wake
As an inevitable consequence.

For you that fly around the world
A ton of fire per thousand miles
Look down and see My images starve
While you wile away your guilty wiles.

While you smile away your guilty smiles
Oxfam's Danegeld your conscience salves
Up here I bile my heavenly biles
Fuck you world and your guilty smiles.

And did My feet in Ancient time.
Walk upon England's mountains green
You bet they did you bet they did
But next time I'll put the boot in, kid.

But soon the tread of pestilence.
From atmospheric consequence
Will over fly My ten mile fence
With disease and death, you malcontents
But will I hear your sick laments?
Or will I close my heavenly tent?
And forget I ever knew you.

Part of the cross of being God
Is to I love bastards such as you
But if I were to have one day off
You'd see what Almighty God could do

I'd fuck you rich that screw the poor
I'd show you what heavenly wrath is for
I'd jam your finger in my door
I'd spank your bottoms till they're sore

I'd crucify each one of you
That play Me and change my world
Ignorant as you daily drive
Around the M25

Ignorant as you fly above
The clouds to New York City
Just remember God is love
God is love and God is pity

Just remember as you burn
The kerosene that makes the engines turn
My omnipotence may change My mind
You may say I'm love defined

But omnipotence can change a definition
Omnipotence can change the course
Omnipotence can make the world a hearse
And cancel your salvation.

So don't read the print on promises made
Believers when you're in your grave
It's me that you rely on.

As you're in My Image made
Know from yourselves what I would do
With smug bastards that push their luck
And undo the good I do.

Don't fuck the world
Don't screw the poor
Remember what compassion's for
For you're in My image made
And you'd rage on
Yes you would rage

If one of your son's saw the other one's daughter
Be murdered in jail and given no quarter,
While calmly continuing the daily drive

Around the M25
Around the M25
Around the M25!

At the Ordnance Survey

I want a symbol for my map
That marks the happy times we had
Placing memories on my desk
Like battle sites or monuments

Another symbol for my map
To site our oneness in the dusk
Dark cold air locking tight
The warm soft bubble holding us

Another symbol on my map
For sites of passion in the sun
The buzzing flies, the musty ditch
Cathedral towers forgiving us

      Romantic of Rochester

Auntie Jayne writes:

> Dear Romantic of Rochester,
>
> You are in luck. David Rhind, the Director General of the Ordnance Survey, has agreed to ask his staff if they could design special symbols, if there is a demand for them, for happy places, loving places and passionate places.
>
> Would any reader who would be interested in buying a personalised memory map circle 998 On the Reader Enquiry Card.

If you are interested in being a potential business partner please circle 999.

I may be jumping to the wrong conclusion about your last stanza but, just in case, I have asked for some theological guidance about acts of passion on hallowed ground. I will contact you privately in due course.

Sunstroke on Ilkley Moor, LS29 2BT

Thou surely won't catch death of cold
And no worms will come and eat thee up
And no ducks will come and eat up worms
So we won't 'all have eaten thee'

Every well-read worm that chews the sod
Knows its postcodes and its neighbourhoods
Its darkest nightmare in its sunless hole
The flat consuming menace from the woods

      Yorkshire Ecologist

Auntie Jayne writes:

Dear Yorkshire Ecologist

Your point is a good one: The changes we are making
to the world, will have many more consequences than
simply making the weather warmer. I like your example
of the New Zealand Flat Worm which is found mostly
in woodland in its native land: It wraps its body round
our native earth-worm to dissolve it into a gluttonous mass
before sucking the goodness out. As you hint, it was a
clever idea Dr Jones of the University of Manchester to
map the flat worm's progress using postcode information.

Learning by Rote

De-DAde-DAde-DAde-DA
De-DAde-DAde-Daaaah-da
De DA-da-da de DA-da-da
De Daaah-da Daaah-da DA-da

The new National Curriculum
Has got us all confused
The Minister of Education's
Going on the Evening News

Our new headmaster Mr Patten
Makes our education happen
Squeeze the older teacher out
For Master Spink and pay him nowt

Sad to say, good education's
Not what we can all afford
So Master Spink our cheaper teacher
Chalks it up upon the board

We must learn it all by heart
And if we scribble very fast
We can write it down again
In the year's exam campaign

We will beat the other kids
Know every line of "Katy Did"
And with our teacher Master Spink
We'll learn to spell, forget to think

We'll learn to spell, forget to think

Auntie Jayne writes...

> Geoffrey. It is you isn't it, following your obsession with exams [*] and how your slow writing speed has blocked your progress - but is this still relevant?
>
> Update yourself on current exam regulations.

[*] <u>Exams and handwriting on faxfn.org</u>

Driving home for Christmas

***

1. **Pope Francis:**
    "Climate change is the road to death"

2. **IPCC (SR15):**
    "Decarbonization ... needed to stabilize the climate"

3. **House of Commons, Science and Technology Committee:**
    "Widespread [car] ownership not compatible with significant decarbonisation"

***

We're driving down the road to death as Armageddon comes
With our very last breaths we drive on and on as ...
                                      Armageddon comes

    With our very last breath on the road to death
    On the road to death with our very last breath

    On the road to death with our very last breath

***

Auntie Jayne (2024) writes:

    Exceptionally, my comments here are purely supportive...

While there are other sources of carbon pollution, pushing us down Pope Francis' "road to death", mass car ownership is one feature that locks high carbon emissions into our everyday lives - even if we all switch to electric cars: Their manufacture causes high emissions and makes us work so hard to afford them. Then we earn enough to fly around the world.

See Planning to be poorer, car free and happier

A Sentence

How can you make sense of a sentence like this?
How can you make sense of a sentence like that?
How can you make sense of sentences like those?

First get your degree in linguistics
And specialise cataphoric and anaphoric references
Then get your doctorate in philosophy
Specialising in Russell's theory of types

A degree costs the same as a house
A doctorate the same as a mansion
If we could save some money on those
We could send me for lessons in scansion

Auntie Jayne(2024) writes:

> In the early nineties when you wrote this, Geoffrey, the cost of a degree may have been the cost of a house. Now, however, house prices have risen so much that they easily exceed the cost of getting a degree, which <u>Times Higher Education</u> puts at £35,000 to £40,000. You can't buy a house for that.
>
> That's unless you can get planning permission for a plot of land and import one of <u>Elon Musk's Boxables</u> But that's an unlikely scenario. Theoretically, you could buy a plot big enough for a house for less than £1000 (at agricultural prices) then ask for permission to build a house on it. ....
>
> But that's dreaming.

The Universe is Holonomic

> Information is a relation
> Between two states of mind
>
> I know your state
> Or
> You know my state
>
> So far, that's fine
>
> It's rather perverse
> That entropy (its inverse)
>
> Depends on one state
> Not on two states
>
> And, of course, the arrow of time
> Makes this a puzzle to be rhymed

Auntie Jayne (2023) writes

> Interesting. That reminds me of something you said about Eric Idle's Galaxy Song. It includes...
>
> > Our universe itself keeps on expanding
> > and expanding, In all of the directions it
> > can whiz; As fast as it can go, at the speed
> > of light, you know, Twelve million miles
> > a minute and that's the fastest speed there is.

Many of the facts in this brilliant song are about right with one serious exception: The universe is actually expanding faster than the speed of light.

How can the Universe expand faster than the "fastest speed there is"?

Even Josh doing his PhD in general relativity doesn't have a good answer to that.

Update:

Josh has now given me an explanation, based on an analogue of two currents in a current bun. As the bun is cooked the space between the currents expands at a faster speed than the currents are moving.

I'm still confused.

How to draw a curve with one flat point

"Infinite elasticities of substitution in strictly quasi convex utility functions - a note"

Well that fooled 'em

Auntie Jayne (2023) writes:

Yes. An interesting example of academic economics.

Park and Ride

I pay my fare, get on the bus
Lurch to a seat, adjust my truss
And see you walking with your dog
Your middle age looks very odd

You stole my soul that summer's night
Now I steal a little back
From hidden thoughts that once I glimpsed
Through fragmentary cracks

A memory looking to my left
Eyes raised to see our time forgot
Perhaps we never really knew
That wooded way to Camelot

      Thriving Grey of York

Auntie Jayne writes:

    Dear Mr Grey

Knowing your demographic class, Superprofiles Lifestyle B "Thriving Grey" and that you live near one of York's Park and Ride Terminals, I have been able to locate approximately where you live: towards the outer edge of postal sector YO2 2.

I see you read Philip Larkin. He was Chief Librarian when I was at Hull University. My French was just good enough to read the naughty bits in the books of the Marquis de Sade that he stocked in his library.

It's funny, but reading such things in a foreign language somehow makes them less shocking.

Nostradamus, the FT and a Pareto Optimum
(A rhyming Iambic Pentameter for 1994)

"The grave threat of a further boost to extremist politics if reform is PERCEIVED to make things worse over the next year means that a substantial rise in open unemployment is now politically intolerable."
                The West and Zhirinovsky,
                Financial Times, 17th December 1993

"Subsidies should not be used to reduce unemployment because they would move away from a Pareto optimum and introduce allocative inefficiency."
                Economist on the Newcastle Train
                23rd December 1993

    The seer saw the tyrant from the East
    Who brings about the ending of the world
    The tyrant gaining succour from the weak
    The listless poor whose voice is seldom heard

    As we approach the ending of the year
    We hope for many joyous years to come
    While in our souls we shrink and cringe with fear
    But thank the Lord our end is optimum

Auntie Jayne (2023) writes:

    Yes economics is sometimes very unreal.
    But who was Zhirinovsky?

Rosetti's Wombat

OK, Robert, You can say
The Pre-Raphaelites were middle-class pratts.

OK, Robert, You can say
That William Morris was a boring old fart.

But don't pull rank with your History of Art.

I can see that like you do.

Yes, today, they'd be drawing
Conan the rebel
Yes, today, they'd be writing
Pretentious drivel

Yes, alright, their poems
Were puerile
Yes, I know, their pictures
Were juvenile

But they were mates
And they had some stories to tell.
They tried to prevent
Our industrial hell

We rush round the world
Screwing it up
When we could be strolling
Their road to Camelot.

> We could be putting our models in baths
> Throwing in flowers and having a laugh
>
> We could write poems and drink lots of gin.
> And could sin and could sin and could sin.

Auntie Jayne (2023) writes:

> Geoffrey, I understand this is one of your older poems. As the BBC often says about the repeats on Radio 4 extra, it reflects the attitude of the time. At least it's not transphobic or homophobic.

"Old soldiers never die they only fade away"
(An old music-hall song)

(To a quick jolly beat. One-two-one-two-one-two.)

> Once there came a regiment a marching down the street. Highly trained technicians, the sort they ought to keep. They sacked all the older ones who'll never get jobs again. And started up a new campaign for young ones they could train.
>
> Once there were some steel workers a walking down the street. They sacked all the older ones, and kicked them in the street. Because of government subsidies, to keep the young ones on.
>
> But subsidies gone, the plant shut down, the young one lost their jobs.

(Bedtime)

> And, children, the happy end to the story, is that grandfather retired at 45 and spent the rest of his life watching TV. Uncle John moved away to an exciting job in Los Angles, where he was shot dead by a mugger, while buying a bottle of Chateaux le Fite, at a seven-and-eleven.
>
> Auntie Jean is coming back to live in Hartlepool because she has a nervous disorder and cannot afford the medical bills over there.

Christine

Stiff and smart, unused pristine
And not for any general use
My prim and proper niece Christine
I never thought could be seduced

Her appetite for culture kept the scruffy boys at bay
She wasn't on for any of that
She thought it wrong to stop and chat
But some Greek boy in some Greek place -
          has brought her into play

Since she yielded up her body
She has gained in style and grace
No longer stiff and sniffy
Love and warmth glows in its place

As her paternal uncle
I keep these thoughts suppressed
But it's hard to meet niece Christine
Without glancing at her breasts

But I will weep for Christine
It was obvious from the start
There's so many fucking bastards
That will break and break her heart

Auntie Jayne (2023) writes:

> I'm pleased you report you do not actually have a niece. OK, some nice rhymes an rhythms but this might damage your reputation.

Firelady

I wait to watch her slide the shiny pole
Her arms and legs forever gripping tight
She seems to slide down into every dream
Her arms encircling me throughout the night

Her strength and warmth and gentlest of moans
My mind at peace and fervour both at once
I feel the place she always used to fill
I haven't had a restful sleep for months

Hanging round the station's double doors
A dirty cold and windy place to be
Reduced to getting distant furtive sights
And wondering if she ever thinks of me

I think she hasn't got another man
I think I'm still the sort she really needs
I think and so in fact I really am
In love with each and every breath she breathes

Auntie Jayne (2023) writes

> I'm not surprised the editor of Mapping Awareness refused this. It was rather naive of you to miss the double-entendre.

Family values USA

Arni Schwarzenegger saved his kidnapped daughter
So they could return to feed the wet-nosed deer
After killing fifty foreign scum by himself

Arni and daughter, as the perfect one parent family could

View the pine fresh valley and streams below
The little girl resumed her role as mother
Cooking cherry pies for her errant son
Made with rectitude and love

Back in Bihac the residents are encouraged
To bear in mind the moral of this dream
Kill to win the right to be American
Arni's friend Robert may soon be President

Aunie Jane (2023) writes:

> I get the general drift of this but who was Arni's friend Robert?

You're never alone with a Strand

(CUE MUSIC)
Dropping his suitcase he leans on an old cart. In the
distance she is approaching along the cemetery track,
lined with trees

    As she walks along the middle of the road
    And as I lounge to strike another cigarette
    She looks straight on avoiding where she knows I stand
    Leaf falls leaf falls leaf falls leaf falls leaf lands

    The falling leaves sound out a rhythm their own
    The cigarette I carefully study in my hand
    The slowest metronome will time the rising smoke
    Leaf falls leaf falls leaf falls leaf falls leaf lands

    As I consume the shiny cold and frosty air
    With poison nicotine and gulps of wilful hope
    She still walks on avoiding where I carefully stand
    Leaf falls leaf falls leaf falls leaf falls leaf lands

    But soon this magic world of ageing celluloid
    Will once again lie silent in its rusty cans
    Still as you sit and watch the credits slowly roll
    Leaf falls leaf falls leaf falls leaf falls leaf lands

    But watch to see the shadow of the scaffolding
    A proscenium from where the leaves were carefully dropped
    This falling curtain keeps me where I always stand
    Leaf lands and lands and lands and lands

Auntie Jayne (2023) writes:

Since reading this I've seen the Third Man again. I can't see the shadow of the scaffolding "from where the leaves were carefully dropped".

However there is something/someone up there dropping leaves. They pile up in the foreground.

The BFI voted it the greatest British film of all time.

An ambiguous cataphoric reference
(What's that? Auntie Jayne)

Inside my skull a cactus grows
Often pricking sometimes flowering

Inside your skull I see a rose
Seldom pricking always flowering

Arise arise arise a rose

But it's still fucking good to be alive.

I shall miss it when it's gone

Condemn a little more

We must condemn a little more
And understand a little less.
We mustn't make excuses for
That lady who screwed the NHS

We must condemn a little more
And understand a little less.
We mustn't make excuses for
That lady who caused such homelessness

We must condemn a little more
And understand a little less.
We mustn't make excuses for
That lady who branded righteousness.

Auntie Jayne (2023) writes:

> I vaguely remember this from 1993.
> Now, I haven't a clue what it's about.

Superprofiles: The Affluent Achievers

We're the Affluent Achievers
The cream that's risen to the top
Living in stockbroker belts
As inner cities start to rot [*]

Sophisticated aspirations
Few monetary cares
The Financial Times our favourite read
To check our daily stocks and shares

Cricket, golf and rugby union
Are the games we like to play
A new posh car to take us on
Another expensive holiday

Subsidised seats for the opera
We regularly use
The Government pays the bills
So we don't have to pay our dues

We all have private health insurance
To guard us from the crowds
Postpone death's sting with vitamins
But we die like anyone else

Auntie Jayne (2023) writes:

[*] I remember being pleasantly surprised by Margaret Thatcher saying "we must do something about those inner cities" after her election victory in 1987.

It took several years to discover that she didn't mean helping the poor people of the inner cities but kicking them out with policies of gentrification. This started a trend that was later continued by the Oxford PPEs of Blair's Labour Government.

One for you, Brian

My garden wall is ten miles tall.
I turn up the heating.

My garden wall is ten miles tall.
I step on the gas.

My garden wall is ten miles tall.
I switch on the factory.

My garden wall is ten miles tall.
And throw over the trash.

My garden wall is half a world wide.
Anybody living on the other side?

Looks as if the weather's on the turn.

Auntie Jayne (2024) writes:

> Even if he was ignorant of the mechanisms of climate change, Brian Readhead was one of the decent ones that fronted the BBC's Today programme back in the 1990s.

Reality - An Ostensive Definition

I always think it rather odd
That ontological considerations
Stop us giving the poor the jobs
To reduce their alienation.

A subsidised train is a real train
You'll find that out if you lie on the track
A subsidised farm is real farm
Arable farmers will tell you that

A subsidised loan is a real loan
To buy mansion, house or even a flat
And subsidised art is real art
But some of us might argue with that

Subsidised trains carry Tory commuters
And subsidised food pays Tory farmers
Subsidised loans pay Tory voters
Subsidised art pays for Tory culture

But subsidised jobs offend Tory thinkers

They'd rather see the poor be poor
They'd rather pay them not to work
It gives them pride to sneer about
The layabouts that skive and shirk.

Pensive of York

Auntie Jayne (2023) writes ...

Geoffrey, I know this is you. Haven't you got a life yet? Still harping on about your policy for labour subsidies paid by rebates on VAT. OK, it might have been a good idea once but it's time you accepted it's not going to happen.

I know you have been on about this since 1969 and got as far as a grant from the European Union to fund Professor Swales' excellent report in 1995 [1] but even 1995 is nearly 30 years ago.

I liked your slogan "Subsidise jobs that use lots of labour. Tax those that don't" but it's time to move on.

P.S. I hope you are ashamed of that first verse? It's awful.

[1] The Employment Effect of Subsidies.

Sub-nuclear Naming

A billion or two
For our next scam.
They've got to believe
It's tomorrows jam.

We've a factor called colour.
We've a factor called spin.
We've a factor called charm.
And we'll count strangeness in.

Sub-nuclear strangeness brings magic to mind.
Sub-nuclear colour to which they are blind.
A charmed life is good life in a sub-nuclear way.
And sub-nuclear spin has metaphorical sway.

Sub-nuclear tackiness.
We've done that before.
Sub-nuclear loneliness?
That's it. I am sure.

It's got the right sense
It's just slightly odd.
They'll think we're looking
For sub-nuclear God.

I think we have cracked it
Don't you agree?
A billion for you.
And a billion for me.

Auntie Jayne (2023) writes:

> I know there was a time when High Energy Physics took an enormous proportion of the UK's science budget but this poem may now be outdated.

They still don't know what they did

A butterfly's flight in the Sargasso Sea
Starts a hurricane that drowns Tennessee.

The butterfly whirrings of architects' thought
Start up movements to screw the world up.

The thoughts start gently with illustrated maps
Some nice axonometrics and pretentious crap

With glossy brochures and charming PR
The builders sell concepts - but never show cars

A good example is slab block flats
Awful as homes, as communities crap.

It would be lovely to put their butterfly minds
In Birkenhead Piggeries or in Hunslet Grange.

Then they'd soon know what they did

Auntie Jayne (2023) writes:

Most hurricanes that hit North America originate in the near-equatorial latitudes off the west coast of Africa, often seeded by disturbances that drift down from the Atlas Mountains in Morocco.

Hunslet Grange multi-storey housing was built in 968. Its demolition began in 1983. The Piggeries were actually in Everton not Birkenhead.

DECAL can map it

    The plug on the wall in the room
    Gives meaning to life at four in the morning.

    But when I awake from my dream
    I remember it all with a sense of foreboding.

    The plug looks the same
    Life's meaning is gone..

and I'm left with this rather silly feeling that the absolutely brilliant thoughts I thought I was having are the more the wanderings of a poor old soul (as grandma would say) than the sharp decisive insights of a razor sharp mind that they seemed to be at the time.

Auntie Jayne (2023) writes:

    Two words: pretentious crap.

Let's Try

"We therefore need a new contract between the state and the citizen. The duty of the state should be to ensure that within a year of becoming unemployed every individual has offers of training and/or work. And the duty of the citizen should be to accept one of a number of reasonable offers."

Richard Layard and John Philpot. FT. 11th Septemper 1991

Rock on, Rock on,
Layard and Philpot.
Rock on, Rock on,
You're out your brains.

The winds of time
Throw in your face
You're cure-it-all
That we should train.

The training's crap
Even when its posh
The trainees cannot
Do the jobs.

A point to note
Is Oxford greats
They've fucked us all
The stupid sods.

> Mock on. Mock on,
> Voltaire, Rouseau.
> The First Division's
> Got us screwed.

Auntie Jayne (2023) writes:

> Geoffrey.
> More of your obsession - and it doesn't
> read well. Put this one near the end.

A New Mission Statement

I'm now a poet
But not very fine
At prosodic structure
Or elegant rhyme.

But I don't care
If I'm not pure.

It's not the elegance
But the violence
I do it for.

But for all those cactuses out there
You've got to admit
I've a better grasp of allusion
Than I once did.

Mission Statement extra

To be as good as Blake at his worst.
And much less pretentious than Elliot

Auntie Jayne (2023) writes:

OK, you're trying to hide your delusions
of grandeur - but fail dismally.

The Real Thing

"The term 'real' applies to uninterpreted theoretical terms that have survived sufficient empirical tests."

What's your test of reality
Taste, Smell or Feeling?
Even the sharpest sensibility.
Sometimes sees itself reeling.

Everything feels real
Everything sounds real
Everything looks real
Everything smells real

Seeing the crack
You ignore and forget it.
Forgetting the fact
That reality's shell
Can split wide open
Showing you truths
You cannot believe.

Later, gripping your sanity you might say.

My theory was wrong
It wasn't the real thing
It was some other thing
Now it has gone.

> But knowing yourself it's only a trick
> Like rubbing your shin at site of the kick
>
> It stops the brain
> Knowing the pain.
> But the ache exists
> And the pain persists
>
> All the same.

Auntie Jayne (2023) writes:

> Since I've heard you sneer at Eliot's
> "Burnt Norton", this shows your hypocrisy.

British Manufacturing Industry.

British Manufacturing Industry
Where it did work we fixed it.

We stopped the apprenticeships
To spite the union bosses

We started up community charge
To tame the looney lefties

We lit up the house price surge
To pay off our supporters

We stopped the apprenticeships
To spite the union bosses

Auntie Jayne (2023) writes:

I'd forgotten how house price rises have been with us for decades:

In the early 70s, the average house price was £4,975 and by the end, it was £19,925. It was during this decade that the gap between average wages and house prices grew wider making homes less affordable.

See Insight Law's analysis in the paper
Have residential property prices always risen?

Let me mention Gary Stevenson here.

Gary is an inequality activist, economist, and former financial trader. In his Youtube channel, Gary's Economics, he tells of how government policies have engineered an enormous transfer of wealth to the rich, particularly via house price rises. Even the middle classes will find it difficult to own their own homes.

The homes will be owned by the rich, who will rent them to poor (and not-so-poor) people.

Set aside

I don't ask much
With a TV to watch

(A prefabs could be good
Good ones were popular
But they had bad politics)

      ***

Grandmother said I never should
Play with the Gipsies in the wood
If I did she would say
Naughty little girl to disobey
      ***

Set aside set aside
We're not short of land
Set aside set aside
Neither is France

Set aside set aside
There's lots of space
Set aside set aside
For the whole human race.

But this bits mine
That bits yours
That bits theirs
That bit's ours

Set aside set aside
Fly away home
Your house is on fire
Your children are gone

Your children are dead
Frozen and stiff
Set aside set aside
Don't you wonder if

We could set aside Surrey
We could set aside Kent
We could set aside Hampshire
We could set aside Gwent

Auntie Jayne writes (2023):

Garbled - needs work.

Set-aside, the policy paying farmers for removing food production from the market was a perfect counter against those who said we must not build on farmland and destroy food production. Now we have to resort to pointing to the wastefulness and climate destruction of animal agriculture

Twenty years of madness thinking I know how to cure unemployment without inflation.

I must be wrong. Mustn't I?
Someone should tell me why.

Then I can lead my life again
As like an ordinary person.

But it still dances in my head
Every time I watch the television.

I know how to stop unemployment
Without causing bad inflation.

Dr Burton said that labour subsidies cannot work because subsidising at 20 pounds per week so many jobs are created that there are not enough people to fill them.

Later he said that the elasticity of demand for labour might not be 1.0 as he had supposed. It was probably 0.15.

Dr Jones Lee didn't seem to listen. God was he rude? But he did have one interesting idea once. Basically...

You can draw a curve with one flat point.
Or in terms economists can understand...

"Infinite elasticities of substitution in strictly quasi convex utility functions"

Roy Jenkins told me that Nikky Kaldor had the same idea. Nikky Kaldor didn't remember.

I met a Swedish whore on a train, with a silver coloured case, going to stay with the judge. She said Nikky, the economist, was a very nice man. She liked my theory and told me to send it to one of her MPs.

I doubt if he read it.

Auntie Jayne (2023) writes:

> Still self obsessed.

Chomsky

So Mr Chomsky.

(very fast)
   At this moment in time I have a picture in
my mind but I don't know how this picture
will come out - no not a picture but a
feeling from a tangle of neurones or rather
a meaning in a web of thoughts -anyway I
have this sensation of understanding I know
what the voice in my head is talking about.
It's looking round these mental object things
trying to somehow get them out

(decelerating)
   in sounds that follow each other.

(clipped)
   You're wrong thinking I think like you think
that you think.

(measured)
   Perhaps the glib, the grammarians, the world-
at-one, two superficial essays a week, Oxbridge
PPEs can use your structures. But I like to
know the weight of the bus, the speed of
sound and how many plastic bags equal a
drive in a car.

   Give me the nouns, give me the verbs (and
the other bits) and I can produce an infinity
(denumerable of course) of concrete

instantiations of your structures.

We could send them to the structuralists for textual analysis.

(sharply)
But when I cross the road it's not the subject or the predicate or their transformations that interests me.

(slower)
It's the weight of the bus.

Auntie Jayne (2024) writes:

In 2024, many of us regard Chomsky as a truth-telling hero but accept his attempt to turn syntax into a model of thought as misguided. It did, however, give him the platform to become a super-star of morality.

A Keller of a Joke

Tony Hancock was The Rebel
He could make it rhyme
Thank you for a style like that
I think I'll make it mine.

But if you don't think it's really ART
Just remember Piotr Zak . [*]

Talking to a composer about his work, Trevor said, "The ear can't tell the difference so why alternate between 13/9 time and 14/10 time?"

"Because it wouldn't be my music otherwise", he said.

Auntie Jayne (2023) writes:

This is a reference to the film, The Rebel.

Hans Keller and Susan Bradshaw, concocted the deliberately unmusical percussive piece as a hoax, pretending to be the "modern music" of composer Piotr Zak. It was broadcast twice on the BBC Third Programme on 5 June 1961.

Memories of Paris II
"Marylin Monroe se tuer"

How was I taken back ten years.
From York to Paris in an instant?

It took half an hour to find a jar of bad garlic.
Subliminally fumigating that hot weekend.

The peaches had smells.
They never do here.
The metro had smells.
Like it doesn't do here.
All Paris had smells
Like it doesn't do here.

(I accidentally brushed the old Prince of
Matter Waves off a pavement in Neuilly.
But he rippled on by.)

The Opera lit-up,
The Orangerie paintings
A boat trip en sewer I thought never would end.

An old monkey tied up and wanking
Two little girls laughing.
My feet hurting to catch my fat friend.

Memphis Slim singing
At Les Trois Maiellettes
The American believing that sob story again

("Ou est la Place Vendome",
  said the American girls.

"Just round that corner".But, expecting
  a reply in French, couldn't understand.
They said "Did you just speak English?")

I want to return. I want to return.
But I've lost my chance.
I should have got out when the clever ones did.
Then I could spend my "Year in Provence".

If I'd sold my house then.
Like the clever ones did.
I could buy Paris.
Leaving mortgage to kids.

Costs of the Psyche

"Our results show that people are concerned much more with inflation and regard the prospects of unemployment quite lightly. American research shows this effect even more strongly."

"But would you say the rise of Hitler was a cost of unemployment."

"What?"

"Well what about ram-raiders in Newcastle. Are they a cost of unemployment?"

"Well I suppose unemployment has its psychic cost." [*]

[*] This is technical economist talk meaning :

> Unemployment can make people unhappy but happiness is not easily measurable, so we mustn't worry about it too much.

The ghost of Albert Speer

These ARE clever people
These people ARE nice
They'd help in a fix
They'd give their advice

But their probit analysis
(And their logit tool too)
Their statistical microscope
 Hides the obvious truth

Focused tightly on figures
In the Employment Gazette
(Or the Expenditure survey)
Their sight cannot reach
Mother's begging with babies
In St James's Park Tube.

Clickety-click, Clickety-click

But further than Epping
In lands not far off
The boots are now kicking
Auslander mit jobs.

Clickety-click, Clickety-click

Can you feel the train rocking
Can you see out the truck
Can you smell the dead corpses
Did you step in the muck?

Clickety-click, Clickety-click

You can see through the crack
Speer's new building at Leeds
New SS headquarters
That's just what we need.

Clickety-click, Clickety-click
Clickety-click, Clickety-click

***

We won't give them job's
We won't even try.
We must always remember that
Arbeit macht frei.

Ordinal Utility

Too serious to Joke
Too pathetic to Believe

"You might say that utility can be measured in the blood. But that would be a measurement of blood not utility.", Lionel Dimwit Robbins

A bad case of Carnap syndrome gone wrong.

Carnap syndrome?

Yes Carnap syndrome.
The one before Popper syndrome.

Popper syndrome?

Yes Popper syndrome.
The one before Kuhn syndrome.

Kuhn syndrome?

Yes Kuhn syndrome.
The one before Lackatosh syndrome.

Oh. I've heard of that.
And they're still suffering from a bad case of Carnap?

It was more like Bridgemanitis.
But they're beginning to recuperate.

Any special treatment?

I think Feyerabenase would be too strong for them. A nice simple diet of Braithwaite's uninterpreted theoretical terms might help. Nothing too taxing.

But I'm afraid it will be along time before they can even begin to talk about the poor being poor and the rich being rich.

Spot the deliberate mistake

NO INFLATION
NO UNEMPLOYMENT
NO POLLUTION

(But possibly a few more taxes for the affluent)

If jobs can be created and pollution controlled with a zero effect on the PBSR, inflation can be squeezed out of the economy by the usual means.

S = Subsidy on goods using lots of labour.
T = Tax on goods using little labour.
D = Savings on the dole etc.
P = Pollution Tax.

Balanced Budget : $S = T + D + P$

S- Creates jobs (mostly for the lower paid).
T- Squeezes capital and the higher paid.
D- A free lunch.
P- Stops pollution.

Further reading: Northern Economic Review No 15. "Employment Creation with Very Large Scale Labour Subsidies".

Deliberate mistake : Public Sector Borrowing Requirement is abbreviated to PSBR not PBSR.

Auntie Jayne (2024) writes:

What a sad story. If only you had avoided green ink.

It ain't the news today, O Boy.

John Peel show. 1.00am news after Bloody Sunday.

>"I'm near the head of the marchers.
>We are approaching some soldiers up ahead.
>My God. They are shooting at us.
>My God. They are shooting at us. "

John Peel show. 2.00am news after Bloody Sunday.

>"I'm near the head of the marchers.
>We are approaching some soldiers up ahead.
>My God. They are shooting at us.
>My God. They are shooting at us. "

A bedroom in Liverpool. 2.01am

>"You won't hear that in the morning."

Today programme. In the morning

>We didn't.

Kincora Boys Home

"At Kincora Boys Home they buggered the boys."
Ken Livingstone, James Whale Radio Show, 1991

        I know they did it
        Thou knowest they did it
        He knows they did it.
        She knows they did it.
        We know they did it.
        You know they did it
        and THEY know ... THEY know ... THEY know they did it.

The Sun, the Stars, the Mail, know they did it
(But the BBC wants its licenced renewed.)

        Ken says they did it.
        But nobody listens.
        Perhaps nobody said it.
        The words were illusions.

So ...
I won't admit it.	(Paranoid me)
Thou won't admit it.	(But thou art naive)
He wont' admit it.	(A Tory MP)
She won't admit it.	(It was HER friends that did it)
We know they did it.	("But don't know for sure.")
You know they did it.	("But not any more").
They know they did it.	(They'll do it again.)

We don't ask questions or make a noise
So at Kincora Boy's home they'll bugger the boys.

Why labour subsidies cannot work

"Labour subsidies cannot work because if you subsidise at 20 pounds per week so many jobs are created that there are not enough people to fill them."

An economist said that.

"A load of shit."

I said that.

"You can be in my dream, if I can be in yours."

Dylan said that.

Auntie Jayne (2023) writes.

>Here we go again. You're so obsessed.

Plymouth, England, the World

Plymouth

>Michael Foot said in 1946 that
>The citizens of Plymouth would
>Have a better life
>In a modern city rebuilt according
>To the Abercrombie plan.

>(Seeing such ignorance on late night TV
>really, really did make me cry.)

The World

>My garden wall is ten miles tall.
>I turn up the heating.

>My garden wall is ten miles tall.
>I step on the gas.

>My garden wall is ten miles tall.
>I switch on the factory.

>My garden wall is ten miles tall.
>And throw over the trash.

>My garden wall is half a world wide.
>Anybody living on the other side?

>Yes.
>But they're dying. It won't take long.

Looks as if the weather's on the turn.

Plymouth

Well Michael are you glad

    Children don't play in Plymouth streets.
    Keeping them safe from modern life?

    The drive in pubs, the supermarkets
    They wonder who their neighbour is.

England

We're rich now but were poor then.
    For holidays we'll fly to Spain.
    We'll fly again.

We're rich now but were poor then.
    Drive to the recycling point.
    Take the plastic bags back.

We're rich now but were poor then.
    Drive the kids to school.
    Water skiing tonight.

We're rich now but were poor then.
    That's why we ram-raid.
    That's why we sleep rough.
    That's why we smoke crack.
    That's why we act tough.

Going underground to beg with our kids.
Refine our techniques to get your spare change.

> If the punters are sitting, go down on a knee.
> If they haven't a pound, then get 50p.
> If they haven't a pound, then get 50p.

Difficult Times

I am going through difficult times in these difficult times
I taste the dust in the doorway as I hear the bells chime

The cold of the stone bruises my bones
I once had a home with a fax and a phone

In this underpass now, this stench I call home
In this underclass now through no fault of my own

The sounds of the traffic skid over the pavement
and bounce round my head I dream of warm baths,
a clean towel, and a soft smelling bed.

When I had work, the pay for ten minutes would pay
for my bread But because I am proud, it takes many
hours to get the courage to beg.

I am going through difficult times in these difficult
times And when I expire it won't be for me you hear
the bells chime.

News of the Symptoms

The News

    BBC TV News. December 10, 1992, 15.00 hrs.

    Three Welshmen freed by the Court of Appeal.
    An English couple are agreeing to separate.
    An English tennis commentator dies.

The Symptoms

    I should feel gratitude at their delicacy.
    Not the panic of the truth being hidden.
    Nor the anxiety of not being told.
    Nor the cold sweat of horrors unspoken.

    But they should know I can take it.
    I adjusted to horror once before.

    My father had closed the back door just as a field
    mouse ran in escaping the cat. The scissor action
    of the door and doorstep cut it in half as it
    wriggled, and soundlessly squirmed.

    I felt sick for a while but recovered.

    So don't worry. I'll be alright.

    I can cope with the thousand pretty girls with
    their legs blown off. I can cope with another
    thousand tons of starved-to-death bones.

So don't worry.
I'll carry on as normal.
I can cope.

But, it won't happen here will it?

Oranges and Lemons

Oranges and Lemons say the bells of St Clemens
I fuck men for money says the whore from Nairobi

Schooling my son so he has a nice life
Grows up and gets work and takes him a good wife

A short life, a quick life, too soon I'll be gone
But my genes will survive and my lineage live on

Here is a candle to light her to bed
Here's the warm chopper to make sure she's dead.

Kent or Mexico?

As I grow old I'll need to find
A cheaper place to end my days

I can't afford the Kentish Downs
On a music teacher's retirement pay

I search the world for a simpler place
And I've just heard the radio say

That Mexico takes prisoners in
And charges (just) nine dollars a day

So will they take in pensioners too
I'll pay quite well if they let me stay

A tequila sunrise every dawn
And a margarita to end each day

Hot sun and dust and buzzing flies
But better priced than Pilgrim's Way

Where skylarks soar to shout their songs
At dusk on peaceful summers days

The hazel trees on Burham Downs
Will rustle as my memory strays

But I must now be circumspect
Eking out my teachers pay

        Careful of Chatham

Auntie Jayne writes:

Dear Mr Careful,

Be VERY careful. Do not rush into doing this on your own. Foreign cultures are pitfalls for the unwary. But you do have an idea that may be worth exploring.

You need a large organisation that has expertise in travel, finance, pensions, insurance, housing, healthcare and, of course, undertaking.

Most of these are found within the Co-operative movement.

Uri

As Uri rolled over, the Great Wall of China
Looked silent and small
Two million metres and one billion tonnes
Seemed nothing at all

Now I want to do it. I want the fame
My marks on the Earth that the space bound can see
I want the world to remember my name
I'll burn up the ozone and set fire to the sea

        Dangerous of Teeside

Auntie Jayne writes :

Dear Dangerous of Teeside,

It is not usually my practice to answer poems of
this sort. Your style is much more suited to the
Literary Review (51 Beak Street, London W1R 3LF).

I dislike over-rhymed verses and I would advise
beginners against waltz rhythms altogether.
However, it is clear that without professional
medical treatment you may be a danger to yourself
and possibly others. If you would like to contact
me privately I will advise you of some organisations
that may be able to help you.

Oh and, I don't think Uri Gargarin could have seen
the Great Wall of China from space.

Superprofiles lifestyle E
The Urban Venturer

Never known to own a car
We keep out of the sun   Superprofiles note:
We ride the tube, eat caviar   Low car ownership
And spend our money having fun

We live in postal district 8
Go to balls in suits and gowns   Superprofiles note:
Every night we stay up late   Enjoy pubs and clubs
In the sparkling part of town

We live in flats and terraces
But frequently take flight   Superprofiles note:
This year we've done the Everglades   Expensive Holidays
And also New Orleans at night

We eat out at the Catacoumbs
We all have good degrees   Superprofiles note:
We are tomorrow's management   Professional
And soar above your jealousies

Travelling by train

Dead or dead-drunk the not-so-old soldier-tramp
was stretchered away. His limp-jointed grubby
dead-weight body heavier than just sleeping

"It's exciting to still be in Thatcher's Britain", I said
Polishing up my best irony.

The man waiting to be served ignored me

Bastard.

Shortly after, the English, don't-get-too-close-to-
anyone principle forced me to set my french
fries and paper-cup coffee opposite him

After a while we talked.

We wondered where they buried these sad ex-heroes.

And commended Camden Council for providing
bins for used needles in the station bogs.

The boat-train from Tramore

The boat-train from Tramore was punctual
But carefully timed to miss the Fishguard boat
So in that time warp of sheer Irishness
We waited seven hours until the next

A forgotten ground sheet and a leaky tent
Had cut short a pleasant sleepy stay
We strolled along the quayside sniffling damp
And stopped to watch the cormorants at play

>Resigned of Rochdale

Auntie Jayne writes:

Dear Resigned of Rochdale,

>Your use of the term "Irishness" smacks of
>residual racism. And as this is a case of
>misaligned timetables it is unfair to blame
>one party. It is true that during early autumn,
>the boat-train, operated by Irish Railways,
>used to arrive after the Fishguard ferry, operated
>by British Rail, had sailed from Waterford. This
>was due to the fact that BR changed to its
>winter timetable sooner than Irish Railways.

Californians (Life Value : $1.5m)

Lying hot in the afternoon doorway
Carl's arm blocked the heat of the sun
His pool of carefully dribbled vomit almost dry

The roar of the traffic drowned passing footsteps
The sun-baked brew of fumes burning his eyes and nostrils
As he tensed himself to keep alert

Looking forward to a shower and evening tennis
He momentarily lost concentration and missed
The footsteps that took his bait

His wallet gone on light young feet
Sprinting away
With 200 dollars of LAPD cash

The backup team across the road screwed up too
They had been distracted by a sudden
Writhing of activity

From the human remains in their doorway

A draft of the forthcoming report from the
Intergovernmental Panel on Climate Change
calculates that there will be five times as many
deaths in poor nations as in the OECD
countries as a result of global warming.

The draft costs the death of an American at
$1.5 million but the death of a citizen from
a "low income country" at $150,000.

Samuel Fankhauser of our World Bank Global Environment Facility is a co-author of the report.

Film Quiz

Looking closely at a wet and slippery print
He can't be sure of what he's really found
And later in the roar of rustling trees
He finds a body shining pallor on the ground

We never know exactly where we are
We're never told exactly what we think
No balls, no end, no place, no plot, no sense
Pretentiousness, a mire in which we sink

Buff

Auntie Jayne writes:

Dear Buff

I know this film. It is a blast from the past. 1967 or 1968? But your question makes me suspect you were just a bit too old to have enjoyed the mental free-fall of the sixties.

Even now you have not learnt to reconcile the analytical and the sensual sides of your character. If the sixties taught us anything it was "Know yourself".

OK, there is little plot, so your security blanket of a simple message is missing. But "roar of rustling" and "shining pallor" shows you are also sensual. And the tennis match at the END may have had no real BALLS but it definitely had a PLACE.

Pearson Professional have kindly provided me wit an aerial photograph of the actual tennis court and the site of the murder. I am posting this image on my web page with the name of your film.

Try searching for it using Alta Vista (http://www.altavista.telia.com) with the key words: "Auntie, Jayne and Blow Up"

Every Body Tells a Story

(An Unsyncopated Iambic Heptameter)

The learned horse can read your thoughts
                    and count them with his feet

Your body movements tell a story
                    every time we meet

I close my eyes and hear the tremble
                    mixing with your speech

But satisfaction doesn't come,
                    the pain goes far too deep

The Convert

Remember Remember the fifth of November

> It was ten o'clock in the evening
> When I was called in for extra duty
> My first week on the job
> I had the job of turning the wheel

Remember Remember the sixth of November

> He held out for hours and hours
> Before the bosses got what they wanted
> He felt bad about ratting on his mates
> And kept asking for forgiveness

Remember Remember the seventh of November

> Sometimes you get cross when they resist
> But this one gave us a good time
> He squirmed and screamed but still resisted
> We thrilled to hear the crack of his joints

Remember Remember the eighth of November

> We had short naps each time he was
> Released to sign his confessions
> But by the end we were
> Triumphant, knackered, tired, released and satisfied

Its an experience I won't forget

But here's one thing that worries me father
I had an erection
And he was a man
Was that a sin?

Exam question 6:

"Analyse the prosodic structure of the text below.[*]
Please use as little technical jargon as possible.
Please do not comment on the semantics."

> I bought a book by Robert Reich
> He tells his story very nice
> The way to make our country great
> Is spending lots to educate
>
> The girl in the bookshop is paying her fee
> Nine thousand a year for another degree
> She's got two already so it's rather odd
> That the bookshop is what
>   she must do for a job

[*]"Dimensions of Prosodic Structure", Anthony Fox. Working Papers in Linguistics & Phonetics. No 4 1986.

Lessons in Politics No. 3

Is There Really "No Proven Link"?

John Hutton MP on behalf of the Dept. of Health in a parliamentary debate on benzodiazepines, states that "there is no proven link between benzodiazepine use and damage to developing foetuses."

<u>Benzodiazepine use and damage to developing foetuses</u>, Susan Bibby, Faxfn.org

Assessment of candidate:

Student: John Hutton MP

Practical Assignment : PQs on Benzodiazapines

Mark: 75%

Notes: John, we all know you're not a lying bastard so why use the old "there is not proven link" line.

The Great British Public still remember tobacco and BSE. Otherwise it was a credible performance.

Green shoots at Canary Wharf

Fax to Today Programme, Radio 4, 071 580 4764

"I'm fairly certain that as the global economy
recovers those office blocks in docklands will fill."

>   Michael Howard, Environment Secretary
>   Today Program, Radio 4, March 25, 1993

>   Microsoft's office will fit in a shoe box
>   And contact the world with the use of a phone
>   So what will they do with the Holborn Bars Site
>   When I run Prudential Assurance from home?

>   That empty office at London Wall
>   Will they fill it with holes like the Albert Hall?
>   And those green shoots at Canary Warf
>   Will they grow in the quiet through
>   the cracks in the path?

Auntie Jayne (2023) writes:

>   That prediction was well ahead of its time -
>   but sending a poem to the Radio 4 programme!

Was it in colour? Green Ink??

Da-di-dadi-Daaaa-da

Plastic bags are dandruff
CO_2 is AIDS
Plastic bags look messy
CO_2 makes storms and waves

To get it in proportion
We shouldn't fly many planes
Ten million plastic bags it takes
To fly the plane to Spain and back.

So forget about recycling
But stop your flying off to Spain.
Go by rail - enjoy yourself
So not to start the hurricanes.

I wonder if Brian Redhead would understand this one. "But", I once heard him say, "won't the Greenhouse Effect be better when we all have catalytic converters?"

"You can't knock Brian Redhead", says Matthew." He's alright really."

Yes, but even the alright ones are so fucking ignorant.

Remembrance

I remember you
Before you remember you

But I remember a week ago
So much worse than you do

But you'll remember me
I hope you do
When I don't remember me a bit

Millennium Bridge (2092)

"Oh my. A hundred today.
And I'm just getting started."

If I had been an ordinary bridge, carrying people across a "motorway" (as they used to be called), I would melt with shame.

I was the cost of five hundred years of human food, when many people starved. It is, of course, the first law of transporters that the well-being of organic life comes before us. In my case that's equitable: I have seen the longest lived animals grow and die in my short life.

I will outlive the longest lived trees on the river. I will stand here in this pleasant place for a thousand years or more.
  (God and the maintenance crews willing).

But my creation marked the changes to the better life. The life where, in summer, the dandelion seeds float down the breeze onto the river and float down the river into the sea, and the people have the time to stand on my broad back and watch them disappear.

My people are not all happy all of the time. A few are not happy any of the time. But it's so much better since the time of the changes

When a place for serenity was found in the world,
When a place for simplicity was found in the world,
When a place for enjoyment was found in the world,
When a place for justice was found in the world,
When a place for happiness was found in the world.

I am proud to have been at the beginning of that.

I listen and watch. I smell and feel.

The children playing in the park.
The snowflakes in my lamplights.
The old men contentedly strolling.
The sun steaming the river.
The splash of the oars of the young rowing their boats.
The snore of their parents lying on coats.
The hiss and the glide of the ducks' landings.
In the dark, under trees, the lovers make my paint blush.
(Carry her gently. Don't let her drop.)

In the morning, the dying looking for things
                                        they remember.
Later, the travellers hurrying to work.

It good to be a hundred. Now I'm growing up.

Now that people have the time ...

to listen to the ripple of the water and
smell the sweet dampness of the riverside.

Billy Butlin

Mummy met Billy Butlin in 1936. She was staying in Dovercourt in Norfolk with her brother Bill who was in the Navy and had just come back from a posting in Hong Kong. Mummy was twenty one and Bill twenty three.

She had just met Daddy who came up for the weekend. She wasn't happy about Daddy coming because Jack Wilson, the pianist, had asked her out.

Billy Butlin was 30+ at the time. He came in a big car and looked handsome and affluent in a light grey suit and a blue shirt. The camp staff were excited to see him. He was already very successful.

Mum and Bill won the dance competition at the entertainments hall where they had a small dance band. She went swimming at midnight in the heated pool and enjoyed late-night floodlit bowling.

A losing streak

He lost the house
He lost the car
He lost the dog as well
He's now wishing on his star
With nothing left to sell

The kids had moved out years ago
His aspidistra died of drought
His cat has died, his bike was stolen
So all he's got is nowt

A pleasant sensation

You flush the bog on the train
At a hundred miles an hour.

You open the window to look for the station
And wipe your face from a refreshing shower

The Empirical Test

The Empirical Test is a series of books of poems or poem-like texts. If you climb the ladder, I hope you see meaning in the title.

This first is "An Economy of Words". It's purpose is to get a few more people to be aware of large scale labour subsidies to create decent jobs for the poor.

Yes, I've written all the bloody poem-like things because I ain't got no satisfaction from the publications I've had so far. And with a little help from my friends some of them were rather good.

But, to my surprise, this has been fun. I'm sure more will follow.

Thanks to Judith, John, Sam, Rachael, Hazel, my kids and their friends. Pete, I hope this doesn't embarrass you too much.

But thanks.

And Mummy, those things you told me when we thought you were dying. They made me proud of you.

Auntie Jayne writes (2023):

"If you climb the ladder, I hope you see meaning in the title."

Even the original of Tractatus was pretentious. But there was more pretentiousness to come when it was turned into an opera by Balduin Sulzer. If you are a connoisseur of pretentiousness get this from TheMusicSalon:

> "The chilliness, alternating with rapid crescendos, with which [the singer] Pammer delivers the philosophical libretto recalls the book's tenor, as well as Wittgenstein's temperament more generally. Given to violent outbursts and fits of derision, Wittgenstein spent the first part of his life attempting to create perfect systems— a logically perfect language."

Was it true he threatened Popper with a poker?

Please forgive much of this.
It's wriggling in pain not viciousness

Possible exception:

" <Redacted>doesn't<Redacted><Redacted> <Redacted> weak at the knees."

Redressin the Balance

Note: ^t =glottowl stop

Le^t us praise God for Estury English
Naer wec'n start to towlk straight
Those dim barstards with Posh Oxbridge Accents
Naer Wec'n see 'em as fakes

Those smug barstards with BBC English
They speak with such authority
But corner them where you can ask em a question
They know less than you do or me

Those crooked barstards with FO type English
Who lie through their teeth as they smile
Their smooth and soft voices hide devious plans
But we can see through their devious guile

And those nice boys with third program voices
With whispers that sound really odd
The Beeb is doing 'em a bit of a favour
For who else'd give em a job

Those verbose barstards with extended code English
(I'm sorry if I'm being snide)
But they're hiding their meanings in wall to wall wordage
Limp meanings we'd all want to hide

Those dim barstards with Posh Oxbridge Accents
The've 'ad it, the're 'istory, forgo^t
For with sharp minds and arh Estury English
Our progress they just cannot stop.

High Energy Physics or
Clean water for the human race

	Cost	Benefit
Little fleas	$1,000	$1,000,000,000,000
have		
smaller fleas	$1,000,000	$1,000,000,000
on their backs to bite em. Smaller fleas have		
lesser fleas.	$1,000,000,000	$1,000,000
And so		
ad infinitum	$1,000,000,000,000	$1,000

Happy End

Hear the
Heartbeat
As much as its
Able

Hear the
Heartbeat
Rocking the
Room

Hear the
Ping Pong
Ball on the
Table

After Birth

I curl into a foetal shape
(Remembering the womb?)
That's why I stop and ponder
On the previous poem.

Does warm and wet
Give better sex?
Or are we still hoping
To be comfortably floating?

Middle Age Stress

Go to bed.
Switch out lights.
Lie on your back.
Wait to warm up.

Hear the sound in your ears.

BShhhh BShhhh
Heartbeat
Sound in your
Ears

Image the sound bouncing across the ceiling

Leffffft right
Heartbeat
Sound on the
Ceiling

Rock your head gently

Hear the
Heartbeat
Rocking the
Room

Hear the
Heartbeat
Sound under the
Table [*]

Goooh tooo Slleeeeep.

Goooh tooo Slleee...eep.

[*]The table tennis table, where I used to hide when I was very young.

Sinning

Forgive me father for I have sinned
I switched off the radio
Forgive me father for I have sinned
I ignored the screams
Forgive me father for I have sinned

...but I'll do it again.

An Infinite Coastline in a Transient World

Monsieur Mandelbrot thought of the fractal
That's what makes him a god

But when I discovered my wriggly curve
I was just thought of as odd

You are my Freudian slip
You are my pavement trip

From the back of the bus I watched you
key into your phone
No longer dialling me but some other

Smug-Oxbridge Bastard

This is generic term.
You can be one of these without having a degree from Oxford or Cambridge.

But the Smug-Oxbridge Bastard ...
will usually have a degree in some Arts subject, like Politics, Philosophy and Economics.

However, my friends John, Simon, Chris, Bob are not Smug-Oxbridge bastards (Physics, Botany, Physics, Physics).Little Johnny certainly wasn't.

Working class origins certainly helps reduce the smugness. Although, as is the case with Trevor, (composition, Oxford) it is not always 100% effective.

Architects, the semantics

'Architects' is a short form for 'successful architects'. The ones that set the trends, who never noticed that the best prefabs estates surpassed any housing done by graduates of the Architectural Association...

"Having lived the first 17 years of my life in [a prefab], this is a real nostalgia trip! I lived in Porters Field Estate in Leyton East London on quite a large prefab estate and it was simply the best community that you could wish for. A safe haven for kids to be left out to play in all day. Hated it when we were all moved out and dispersed into tower blocks or low rise flats....Happy days!"
Tony Perryman,
Customer Review on "Palaces for the People, Prefabs"

Back in the 1960s

I'm looking for my copy of OZ
That shows Germaine Greer's tits
She unzips Vivian Stanshall's fly
Who doesn't seem to mind a bit.

Repeal the Safety Act

When we became the government in 1979
The whole British economy began terminal decline

The unemployed and underclasses are feckless little yobs
So we'll cut their benefits to force them into proper jobs

We know now that British industry is in an awful fix
So we'll repeal the Safety Act of 1936

We're tired of paying for the health care of the rest
So we'll plan a subtle policy to screw the NHS

We must condemn a little more
                            and understand a little less
But, of course, we'll make excuses for
                            those that got us in this mess.

How it is

I like to tell it how it is
But look over my shoulder
I like to tell it how it is
And it isn't the lawyer

I like to tell it how if is
And it isn't my mother
I like to tell it how if is

But will that priest read it?

At least ...

Grannie is dead
Annie is dead
Daddy is dead.
They won't be offended.
But somehow I still worry

... about what they would think.

Idiots

A computer is a high speed idiot - British Council spokesman.

A computer is a high speed idiot - Professor of Vox Pops and Mathematics.

A computer is a high speed idiot - BBC Science Correspondent.

Now we know.

Body Shape and Sporting Success

A Thesis for The Department of Sports Science

(Unfinished)

Colin remembered the junior footballers' mile

They puffed round Wembley's pitch
Before the start of the FA cup
Their short fat legs thumping the ground
Sending dangerous shock waves up
                        to their brains

Not like distance runners at all

                ***

Jacqueline, stayed that summer in Colin's street

    Her French long-legged swaying gait
    He could measure for hours on videotape

His chapter on cycling was his downfall

He simply wanted to know by heart
The names of the towns in the Tour de France

Her body was his *aide de memoir* ..

He placed the start at the nape of her neck
Other names in places he wouldn't forget

She faded from Colin's life with
        the drifting leaves of autumn.

But

    He remembered her Paris
    He fondled her Lille
    He kissed her Calais
    And is cycling still

God's (self) Indulgence

I'd rather let that thief into heaven
Even if he did steal the peach

For I've had my fill of self righteous bastards
Who say

      Speak when you're spoken to

But if I'm in his image and God's like me.
His vengeance might subside.
And look for some practical solution.
And let a few of us survive.

Death of Lennon

OK, Judith, you were right
The rainbow does have seven colours
Because Newton was a Mason

OK, Judith, you were right
The quality of mercy is not not strained through a sieve
The quality of mercy is not not strained to breaking point

OK, Judith, you were right
The quality of mercy is not not strained like that
The quality of mercy is simply not (con)strained.

But, I'm still sure that
Lennon's death was spooky.
Just like Robert Kennedy's.

He was screwed up.
He was ruthless.

But

a) He might have given Peace Yet Another Chance.

b) They were just winning the war against the
thickos in the military when Lennon forced
Nixon to concede the other war to the Vietcong.

> They knew that.
> (So did they act?)

Julie Andrews

Julie Andrews sure turns me on
(A bit of personal conditioning that)
I wish I'd seen out-takes from her SEXY film
Has the director got them back at his flat

But "dew-drops and kittens and ear muffs and mittens"
These aren't a few of my favourite things.
But when SHE sings THAT song
I still get turned on.

But when Coltrane plays THAT tune
I float in a heaven
I feel so secure
He's so very clever
(Playing that naff tune)
Something's inside me I don't understand.

The answer to unemployment, the universe and everything!

The answer

> Subsidise goods that use lots of labour.
> Tax those that don't.

Holding my hand up

> Please miss. I know the answer miss.
> Over here miss. Don't miss me again miss.

With resignation

> Banging on the doors of credibility.
> It's so hard to get taken seriously.

But you have to laugh

> Is that taken seriously from behind
> Or taken seriously from in front, ducky?

"Everybody knows somebody killed in a car crash"
OR
What we see is what we think.

A dance at the Royal Oak, 1959

    I was handsome then, but too dim to know it.

    Judy Lingham sat on my knee most of
            the evening.
    I couldn't stand when she got up.

    But, being gauche, I went home when
            she went for her coat.
    It offended her and I missed my chance.

Exhibition of Roy Lictenstein's paintings, Chelsea School of Art, 1966

    "Everybody knows somebody killed in a car crash".
    One of his best.

    Judy Lingham was killed the day before
    her friend was to be married.
    A car crash on Bluebell Hill.

Reading the Kent News, On the train, December 15, 1992

The inside page had a ghost story.

"The ghost is believed to be that of Judith Lingham who died aged 22."

Question: "Can she still sing alto in the Messiah?"

Memo to the linguistics department

When I start to say a sentence
I don't know what the ending is.
I don't want to sound too pretentious
Or have an intellectual tis.

But if you're all so fucking clever
(Better than ram raiding yobs)
Why, with your transforming grammar,
Can't you get a sodding job?

Those that haven't had advantage
Might just deserve some sympathy
Not you, you lower middle classes
With your limp useless degrees.

Auntie Jayne (2023) writes:

> Geoffrey,. You once told me that the cleverest computer programmer you ever knew (apart from John?) failed his linguistics degree. I suppose this gives a little support to your theme.

Twenty nine, Twenty nine

It's a sign. It's a sign.

Now then Mikey, sweetie dear
I'm not the one to snigger or sneer
If your superstition's 29
That's your sign. That's your sign.

For I walk between the cracks
My fingers crossed behind my back
Count the magpies by the track
Along the railway line.

One for sorrow
I usually beat.
Two for Joy
Who I rarely meet.
Three little girls
No longer little.
Four big boys
Two of them pickled.

Five for the silver
Six for the gold

Seven for the secrets
I never have told.

Some secrets I'm told.
Some secrets I guess.
Knowing too many
That I still must suppress

Knowing too many
And being in some.
Helplessly watching
Just looking on.

It's too late now

OK so you made a mistake

Everybody's entitled to one mistake

But it's a pity it was such a big one

Crossing to the other side

"Orpheus from my Underworld"
A pretentious but memorable film.
Liverpool Film Club. 1969

XMJ 979?

An attractive girl.
Looking round nervously.
As though escaping.

XMJ 797?

She hadn't watched the film.

XMJ 979?

He looked a spotty youth.
Was he following?
I stared. He went.

XMJ 797?
The shop doorway in Bold Street.
She frightened and hiding?

XMJ 979?
The green van slid slowly past.
The driver looked carefully.

XMJ 797?
I took down the number.
But can't quite remember.

XMJ 977?
Too polite to intrude?
Too frightened to help?
Imagined it all?
Imagined it all?

XMJ 779?
A whore on the run?
You know the one.
You know the one.
Murdered and done.
Murdered and done.

(Note for researchers).

I think her name was Anne. On the run from pimps in London. She came back to Liverpool. A careful researcher will find reports of the case in the Daily Telegraph in 1971.

Memo to the Principal

Our staff development newsletter.
Is on incredibly shiny paper.

Stiff enough to make a sickbag.
Dear enough to buy some books.

Our staff development newsletter.
Is on incredibly shiny paper.

It teaches us to arse lick.
But you'd cut your bottom wiping it.

Liverpool lullaby

Do you recall that night you sat
Above the graveyard in the crane
While back at home your good friend Jack
Put in his head and turned on the gas

You climbed the crane
You heard the wind
You smelt the sea
You saw the lights on Heaven's door
Across the Mersey on the Birkenhead shore.

From that crane
To the wind you'd shout.

Can anybody out there
Work any of it out?

Can anybody out there
Work any of it out?

Tate Gallery to Portobello Road is 6 miles

Full of child, a week to go
She trudged along the Portobello Road
You left her at the Tate to walk a long way home
Because Turner didn't turn her on

Was it you who persuaded Jack
To leave her there
For the awful sin
Of rejecting your cultural aspirations?

Did she confront your inner being?
Propped up by your mystical yearning for timeless art

Housing Bingo

A new form of living
To just lie in bed
All I can hear is the rhymes in my head
All I can hear is the rhymes in my head

Herr Docktor, Herr Docktor
Am I really sick
When all I can hear
Is that clickety-click?

It started on Tuesday
And won't go away
My head wakes up buzzing
(And I still hear it sounding)
All through the day

Clickety-click, clickety-click
Clickety-click, clickety-click

I see it, I see it
Grey people are scared
I hear it, I feel it
But I swim with the herd

West Side Story

Everyone's mad in America
Everyone's mad in America
Everyone's mad in America
They shoot each other with guns
Driving round in circles as Armageddon comes.

Recommended reading:

> Mad in America, Robert Whittaker
> "Bad Science, Bad Medicine, and the
> Enduring Mistreatment of the Mentally Ill"

Time has lost its meaning

Time has lost its meaning
Did we ever know that meaning, love?
But still I think I know when
Time held meaning hand in glove

Parmenides

"Nothing cannot be ...
Therefore reality is spherical."

I met a man upon a train
Who hated him as much as me
Next morning in Copenhagen
When I awoke I wasn't free

> Of Rage
> Of Hate
> Of Bile
> Of Spleen

That Thursday night I'd spent in dreams

Of revenge on Parmenides
And the modern kind
Of the clever spoken stupid ones
Who to speak in far-to-clever rhymes.

I am wildly in a rage
I will go and find his grave

> I'd dig him up
> I'd grind his bones
> I'd throw the dust
> Into the flames

I realise that's not enough
To pacify my anger - yet
His timely death
At least two thousand years before
Has paused his subtle wickedness

But he left behind a trail for them
To follow with deft cleverness
To show how argument can suppress
The truth before our eyes.

Philosophers - the essence

by **Jack and Danny**

Wittgenstein

You say something.
I say something.
You guess what I mean.
I guess what you mean.

This was well worth saying.
But apart from this no-one can guess what he meant.
We guess that's how he meant it.
Too clever by half.

Rawls

Everyone should have the same.

No extra points for being beautiful, skilled or clever, but extra points are allowed for good deeds.

Nozick

What's mine is mine.

Taxation is slavery. But paying someone 1 cent an hour to swim in shit isn't.

Nietsche

No-one is in a position to tell you what to do.
So here's what do.

Berkley

Don't look now. It isn't there.

Logical Positivists

Statement a:
    The only statements that have *meaning* are those that can be tested.

Statement b:
    Statement (a) has no *meaning*.

Popper

Statement a:
    The only statements that are *scientific* are those that can be falsified.
Statement b:
    Statement (a) is not *scientific*.

Note: Commonly thought of a philosopher, Popper was really a second rate barrister. Falsification "theory" was simplistic and didn't work and Arthur Koestler thought of it first anyway. But he did give Lakatos a job once.

Scruton

Government Health Warning.
Moral philosophers can damage your health.

Kuhn

Wow man. This particle that's a wave and this time that slows down are so MIND BLOWING that no-one before can even begin to understand where we're coming from.

The old ideas are so dated they
           DO NOT COMPUTE.

PHLOGISTON man, what the fuck's that!

Post

Phlogiston is negative Oxygen.

Jack

Philosophy is Crap.

Danny

Philosophy is Great. Philosophers are Crap.

Heigh Ho, says Roly
(February 20, 1993)

Dear God,

Jerry Adams
Asked me
Over
Today.
So did
Ian Paisley.

Please let me
Tell them
To forget
About You
Just for
Twenty years
Or so.

There's always a way to earn a living

We must not forget, we should know it well
The labouring poor have bodies to sell.

One kidney will do.
They don't need two.
If it's blood that they seek
They can sell twice a week.

One eye's good enough
For watching TV.
Depth vision's for those
Who need it to ski.

Why not become a surrogate mother
Then you won't be a burden to others.

Lump of labour

"If we can imagine a point at which all the necessaries and comforts of life shall be produced without human labour, are we to suppose that the human labourer is then to be dismissed to be told that he is now a useless encumbrance which they cannot afford to hire."
                Robert Owen

"The most frequently recurring scare in world economic history is sometimes dignified by the name " lump of labour fallacy".It is based on the idea that total output is fixed, so that if fewer workers are needed in one line of activity they must end up on the scrap heap."
                Samuel Brittan, Economic Viewpoint,
                Financial Times, February 18, 1993

So Robert Owen.

>You are a
>Lump of labour
>Bonehead.
>
>Everyone else
>Knows
>That total
>Output
>Isn't fixed.

But it might
Just
Stay
Stationary.
Mightn't it?

In my case
It's going
Down
And down.

I eat less.
I rest more.
I don't drive my car
Any more.

A fading photograph

In the fading photograph
Lillian's husband Bill
Looks away from the camera

He didn't want his left glass eye
To be recorded for posterity

For years now I have looked
Eastwards in the sky
To keep my best side
Facing geostationary orbit

Recently a friend has told me
That the orbits are polar
And they only look downwards

Can they see my bald spot?
          - Worried of York

Auntie Jayne writes:

Dear Worried of York,

For all practical purposes your friend is correct as the most publicly available satellite images are from polar orbit. Landsat, the best known, has a resolution of 20 metres. Slightly better resolution can be obtained from the French Spot Satellite. So unless you think you are being targetted by specialised military satellites, you should not worry.

In any case, many women find baldness attractive.

The Boat Show

The Boat Show 1997 for Mapping Awareness

Their boat held still and shining on the sea
They watched the twinkling bubbles from below
From shoals of plenty passing by their shore
The quietness stretched to reach the evening's glow

Taking junction six we made good time
To bring our pleasure craft to put on show
These boats will circumnavigate the world
Our gadgets tracking every wave they go

I bubble gasps like mermaids in those bowls
Happy that we came here to impress
Selling riches to the richest on the earth
But I'm here on swollen feet and gasp for breath

   Trevor from Truro

Auntie Jayne writes

Dear Trevor

I have held back your poem to coincide with GIS 97: I do know the swollen feet and gasp for breath. I too have heard that Cornish fishermen would watch for bubbles from shoals of herring but now we seem to need the most sophisticated of gadgets to detect any herrings at all. I'm sure it's not your fault, Trevor, but our consumer society ... (pompous waffle deleted, ED)

One way bulimia

hungry hungry hungry sick
my feeding frenzy goes too quick
if only i could sometimes stop
to let my hungry-meter flop

hungry hungry hungry sick
the little crumbs i even lick
but now my feeding frenzy's gone
guilt and shame will linger on

hungry hungry hungry sick
i don't remember eating it
i saw it there and now it's gone
self-image nought, the frenzy one

Messages on the Millennium Bridge

We come to celebrate this next millennium
With this bridge to last a thousand years
A bridge of passage and of lasting record
To mark in steel and stone our hopes and fears

***

Since they started off this past millennium
With me, the bridge to last this thousand years
I've seen their happiness, I've seen their sorrow
And eavesdropped on their joys and tears

Each passing season I have kept a record
Of chosen travellers and from whence they came
I preserved their purpose and their destination
To measure how humanity has changed

The summer waters gently flowed beneath me
As lovers idly strolled their time away
Their individual lives passed by me briefly
As I remained to document their strays

***

Four thousand seasons leave four thousand messages
These records on my sides make me complete
And now another bridge is put beside me
For another thousand years of passing feet

About time too

Inside your head a cactus grows
Often pricking sometimes flowering
Let's root it out to plant a rose
Seldom pricking always flowering

He was born in York - but didn't stay

Here is the junk mail crossing the border
With a credit card offer and an Amazon order
Brochures for the rich
Summons for the poor
And a blow-up doll for the man next door.

Here's a stretch limo crossing the border
Carrying its wealth through social disorder
We hide behind glass
And bulletproof steel
Our bodyguard Brad so sure at the wheel

And there is the air-freight crossing our border
Burning the fuel to make the world warmer
Beans from Nairobi
Games from Japan
The World Bank says "Now that's a fine plan"

Now we are approaching our final border
We're getting out because we can afford a
Farm in France
A villa in Spain
From a property deal with significant gain

But here's a nobody not crossing a border
He and his kin ARE social disorder
Nothing to sell
They'll stay in their squats
As the newcomers come and take up our slots.

Auntie Jayne (2024) writes:

" They'll stay in their squats" seems to anticipate the excellent ideas of David Goodhart about "somewhere people" and "nowhere people".

See "The Road to Somewhere", David Goodhart. "The New Tribes shaping British Politics".

MacNeice pastiche

It's no go the electric fire
It's no go wood on the Baxi
Oh for the time when the throbbing heat
Was a bit of skirt in a taxi

It's no go the polar bears
They cannot fly to Iceland
It's all defrost for the whole damn world
And that won't be a nice one

The glass is rising hour by hour
Now it will rise forever
We haven't broke the bloody glass
We've broke the fucking weather.

There's no place like home

Honest John, be honest
Your lads are dim and crap
They'll knock down solid houses
To put up soulless flats.

Honest John, be honest
You've let history pass you by
You've seen it all in Hull before
You of all should know the score
Don't give us more and more and more
Of dreadful dwellings in the sky.

        Slumby Dweller

Auntie Jayne writes:

Dear Mrs Dweller,

Before I get too involved in your subject matter, let me give you some poetic advice. You have managed good rhymes (not so perfect as to be embarrassing) and a good rhythm that varies just enough. I do like the crescendo in the last stanza. The reader can imagine you standing next to Mr Prescott and shouting in his ear.

It may be asking too much, but I should have preferred some sense of the homeliness of your own home in your own street and the soullessness of most modern "social housing units".

And yes, the Office of the Deputy Prime Minister does use that term.

See, for example, the government's publication Spending Review 2004: Press Notice 20 "Housing and Sustainable Communities". (Unbelievable!)

On the topic of housing provision there are these websites:

www.prefabsareforpeople.org.uk
www.greeningthegreenbelt.org.uk

Another Tempest

The captain was as vicious as nails in a bomb
With a rage against the world
He could not contain

But in the quiet of the eye of the hurricane
He called us on deck
To recover our composure
After eight hours of force twelve winds

He made us lie on our backs
Beneath the evening sky
To look at the ancient stars
Through the clear column of falling atmosphere
Squeezed and warmed as it fell

Our circle of peace trapped by the wall of death
Fuelled with air moistened
By weeks in the tropical sun
Which released its steamy heat to swirl around
The rising vortex of force twelve destruction

The condensation first sweating
Then dripping like a cold bus window
Then roaring like a broken sluice
"If by your art my dearest father, you have
Put the wild waters in this roar, allay them."
The Captain shouted

But he knew it was too late

And in his mind he was content to watch
These whimpers at the end of a world
That had pained him too much

With its indifference

Seaman Staines

Auntie Jayne writes:

Dear Mr Staines,

First let me point out your alias comes from a well worn urban myth. Seaman Staines was not a character in the children's television series Captain Pugwash nor was Roger the Cabin Boy . This is clearly explained here.

Secondly, your captain sounds like a pretentious misanthrope to me, one of those selfish sorts who don't do much good so they rail against the state of the world to soothe their own consciences.

Anyway, I have answered your poem because you have described the inner workings of a hurricane rather well. But I'm getting a bit fed up with analysing global warming and related topics. This may be the last one. For those of you that are really interested you can look on the website of the US Government's Geophysical Fluid Dynamics Laboratory.

As the Earth warms it predicts
    some increase in hurricane intensity

But get a life! Next time send me something you really know about. Describe the best brothels in the ports you have visited: A critique of their hygiene standards would be most interesting.

Take it from the Kop

It's such a shame that hapless Tony
Has to smooch with Berlusconi
For us that stand here on the Kop
In this town that time forgot
This sad betrayal hurts allot

It's not because his politics stink
That makes us old stalwarts shrink
But can the tyrant of Milan
Who bends the rules because he can
Be loved by any Liverpool fan

                Scouser

Auntie Jayne writes:

Dear Mr Scouser,

First let me say I don't necessarily accept your alias as accurate. "Such a shame" is not a term commonly used amongst Liverpool supporters - they are typically much more expressive.

I quite like the "hapless Tony - Berlusconi" rhyme but I suspect this has led you to overdo the insult. But if you want your poems to sound less like doggerel don't rhyme so often and, as a learning exercise at least, use Shakespeare's favourite rhythm - the five-beat line.

You will see that changing

>A cart, a horse, a cat, a dog.
>A rat, a cat, a mouse, a frog.

to

>A cart, a horse, a cat, a dog, a mule.
>A chair, a man, a cow, a log, a stool.

makes the lines so much more magisterial.

BBC discovers global warming

The snows of Kilimanjaro are almost gone
The dreamy Maldives drowned and overrun
The polar bears will have no place to roam
They'll lounge their listless lives on solid ground

Casting storms across the Gulf of Mexico
Will God's true aim hit Mickey Mouse and Co
Or will countless sad old dreamers rue the day
When the brothels of New Orleans are blown away

Once leashing weathermen to their tekky lot
The BBC now scorns the lure of academic Philip Stott
Hallelujah, Global Warming is discovered
Weathermen rejoice, their cage uncovered

    Hot under the collar in Tunbridge Wells

*] See Professor Stott's blog EnviroSpin Watch.

Auntie Jayne writes:

    Dear Mr Hot,

    Thank you for giving me the opportunity to criticise your poem. Sadly, your third verse shows an unfortunate chip-on-the-shoulder prejudice. Not all academics are *purely academic*, some of them break free of the constant grind of having to spread one good idea over many publications.

I will try to find out if your contribution can be posted on www.smugbastardsatthebeeb.org.uk, a pleasant lot, if a bit wacky.

I liked you first verse.

Aunie Jayne (2024) writes:

> Geoffrey, you tell me that this was written in 2004 before Hurricane Katrina in 2005.
>
> Really?

Flagellation for poets

Every poet must have a tortured soul
To motivate the flow of reeling words
But sense must keep the torture in control
No broken bones or screams that can't be heard

The lingering pain which stimulates our thought
The dozen thorns that penetrate our minds
Ecstatic, holy, soulful, overwrought
Forget mild spanking on our bare behinds

Trying to be Brave

Held firmly in the spectre's chair but falling fast
Gargantuan smiles that swirl all motion to a stop
The booming voices chasing consciousness from sight
The glaring brightness left behind me as I drop

First the steady rush of breath and cooling air
Then the sickly sweat upon the freezing brow
The shiny floor feels oh so comfortable and soft
The weakened body craving sleeping here and now

This urgent panic haunts me from the distant past
And now a lower molar causes me distress
But when I fight past pain and horrors that have gone
Where can I get a dentist on the NHS?

    Desperate of Doncaster

Auntie Jayne writes:

  Dear Desperate

  Your description of having gas at the dentist shows your age - modern dentistry is much kinder. But it used to be a very unpleasant experience. I know several people who, as children, were sick and fainted at the dentist.

  The British Dental Association advise people that are looking for a dentist to try to find one through personal recommendation.

But, failing that, your local Health Authority should be able to tell you which dentists are taking on patients in your area.

Change of syllabus

I used to make them learn the names by heart
The map spread out across the classroom wall
The Empire where the sun could never set
Now has Gibraltar, Falklands and Rockall

India has gone and Kenya too
As I colour out possession one by one
Australia joins the new Pacific rim
The sun will soon be setting on Hong Kong

Now the map upon the wall has changed
It's Ancient Rome whose glories I extol
Learning every date and every name
Gives them a sense of order and control

        York Schoolmaster
        (Geography and History)

Auntie Jayne writes:

    Dear Schoolmaster

You seem to be unaware that maps are only approximations to reality. You would be much better getting your pupils to examine the differences between London Underground's diagrammatic map and the routes shown in the London AtoZ. Or as a history teacher you might like to use one of your older maps and find out how the quality of life of the indigenous population changed when the map was coloured red.
But I suppose that seems a bit wishy-washy and
liberal to you: better stick to 'the facts' and avoid too much

thinking.

On a conciliatory note I think we were both dismayed when the site of Emperor Constantine's headquarters in York was vandalised to build that office block. I have met the archaeologists that had to scrabble through the skips of rubble to find out what they could.

One performance only

We'll fly you over burning forests
We'll walk you through the starving hoards
We'll show you drowned and bloated corpses
At a price you CAN afford

You'll glide above the sky in comfort
You'll sleep your nights in quiet hotels
You'll sit and watch our views in comfort
Of people in a billion hells

Arma G Heddon

Auntie Jayne writes

Dear Ms Heddon

I am not going to dismiss your project as fin-de-cycle lunacy. This is so often done by commentators ignorant of the science and technology of possible environmental dangers.

This is where the GIS community could help decision makers and opinion formers. Where are the maps explaining the possible role of methyl hydrate deposits in climate change? Or maps showing the geography of world-wide carbon dioxide generation? But I have recently met two different consultants mapping terrorist threats to wealthy people in London, for insurance companies. But as no-one owns the Ozone Layer it cannot be insured!

A call from a daughter (1998)

"The swaying lights are drilling through my head
The giddy rocking's bringing on a retch
Completely lost and don't know where I am
The arm rest's digging deeply in my neck"

Fretful father

Auntie Jayne writes:

    Dear Fretful

    Thanks for your e-mail. I am sure by now your daughter is safe and well and possibly even recovered from her hangover. In future she should get a cab home when she gets drunk rather than the tube.

    But your ditty gives me the opportunity to ride a small hobby horse of mine. Wouldn't if be nice if we had a good desktop mapping facility and geographical search engine to help us in these situations. If your daughter's mobile were fitted with a GPS capability it would then be easy to track her down and arrange for her to be picked up at the next station.

Daughter writes (2024):

    It was me lolzzzzz (although fits for both of us!)

    Got to say dad you were ahead of your time with the GPS stuff!
    Xx

Not my cup of tea

I have never crossed the association's chair
I have never laid down drunken in the street
I have voted with my party all my life
It's geography that's lost my cherished seat

Those commuters on the other side of town
Will elect my most disreputable friend
He has more vices than the singers of the songs
But hypocrisy will get him in the end

    Somewhere in the South East

Auntie Jayne writes:

    Dear Mr Somewhere, MP

    Aren't you bitter! You feel it is the Boundary
    Commission rather than your constituency that will
    vote you out. But they have rules which do not take
    types of voter into account.

    There is no consideration of wealth, lifestyle etc.
    However, other geographic considerations do have
    weight. For example, the Isle of Wight is under-
    represented with one MP but it does not make
    geographical sense to allow the surplus voters to
    vote in Southampton..

    I would be very careful about any allegations you
    make. We may suspect that some MPs do have
    expensive drug habits, although Noel Gallagher is

probably safe from being called to the House to apologise for his "cup of tea" speech, accusing MPs of drug taking.

I like your hexameters.

Betrayed

You're the loved one he won't speak to
You're his love he's shutting out
He's angry and he's childish
His pride has had too strong a clout

He doesn't want to see you
He doesn't want your things about
But he strolls the lanes you wandered
You're his love he's shutting out

A friend of a friend

Auntie Jayne writes:

Dear friend of a friend

My worst failing as an agony aunt is trying to be a bit too clever but it is so obvious you are this childish and angry person. But you have made a good start in understanding your problem - and written two strong stanzas.

I do not know the extent of the betrayal but it does seem that your loved one is asking forgiveness. As Valentine's day approaches you might force yourself to send her a card that symbolises the good things you shared.

Why not send one showing the "lanes you wandered" on it. Mike Squibb of Ordnance Survey Special Products suggests that their

Pathfinder Series would be the best maps to use.

Alan Pease in his book on body language demonstrates that "going through the motions" can affect your underlying mood. So try pretending and see if you can keep it up long enough to replace jealousy and anger by love and forgiveness.

Back from the hills

I wake amongst the chimney pots
I stroll to work through city streets
I warm the night in bars with friends
Then strolling home to clean cold sheets

I sneer at country dwellers all
Who drive to work from heated homes
They pollute the world with affluence
And warm it up for aeons to come

              City Dweller

Auntie Jayne writes:

Dear Robert

I know it's you! You get your chance because this month's postbag has been rather empty.

There is some truth in what you say: Most country dwellers do drive their cars more and stay in heating their homes. They probably do contribute more to global warming through excessive energy use. But it will need some mental adjustments to accept that living it up in crowded city bars and restaurants is lifestyle that the environmentally aware must follow.

It's got that "Save water. Bath with a friend." feel to it.

I have recently seen a research proposal to look at lifestyles and draw maps which show the variability of environmental sustainability throughout the country. But if any reader knows of other work on environmental sustainability and life styles, could they contact Robert Collins c/o City Dwellers, Cappuccinos, Church Street, York.

Auntie Jayne (2024) writes

> Good news. We now have the excellent website Carbon.Place, which estimates the carbon footprints of residents of each Census Output Area in England.

Help !

The freaks on the phone won't leave me alone
I get them from every town
Can I trace back their calls to map on my walls
To help me to track them down

                Harassed of Surrey

Auntie Jayne writes:

Dear Harassed

Your dreadful rhyme brings back a powerful memory for me. Back in the sixties, visiting some smug art school types, I was dragged into leaving silly messages on John and Yoko's answerphone.

They had recorded a rather nice "Welcome to Wonderful Weybridge" song but my companions sang an awful "Yoko, Oh no!" refrain after recording a boring story. I still cringe when I hear John's "freaks on the phone" line.

Crop Circles

We hear the gentle crack of bending corn
We smell the warmth that rises from your hills
In summer nights we execute our art
To show your world our higher alien skills

Our symbols are Bernice's magic forms
So just your cleverest will know
Our higher purpose in our messages
And help your simple culture grow

> Extraterrestrial Extra Intelligence

Auntie Jayne writes

> Dear Extraterrestrial Extra Intelligence
>
> You do not fool me! No advanced culture would be so nerdish as to use Bernice Mandelbrot's fractal patterns as a means of communication: They are, after all, just extra wriggly lines.
>
> You nerds almost certainly come from some university department within a few hour's drive of Stonehenge. Mr and Mrs Taxpayer may one-day want to know what on Earth you are up to.
>
> It is time you were stopped so I have been exploring the possibility of using satellite photography to track you down. Unfortunately most commercially available images do not have sufficient resolution: Landsat's resolution is 30 metres, Spot's is 10 metres.

I am told that some Russian satellites are available with 2 metre resolution and cost about £100 for a 30 Km square. A budget of a few thousand pounds should see our detective work started. I am willing to put in the first £100.

Would readers please contact me if they want to join in.

Rickshaw Ride II

After a drunken night somewhere in Malaysia

When the soldiers sobered and realised
The unattended rickshaw
Was the best way to get back to barracks

Charlie stripped to his underwear,
Trying to imitate a rickshaw driver.
He pedalled his mates back to barracks
Changed into his uniform outside the gates
While his mates

       Disposed of the rickshaw in a storm drain

Back in Edgbaston, he sometimes told that story
But, as the years passed, the remembered thrill
Of a crime shared
Waned

And the memory of that night's stars
Continually moving ahead of them
Faded

He thought less about his mates
And more about the rickshaw driver

Mouthing through the windows

We are pacing up and down the broken train
We are mouthing through the windows, "Let us out"
The smiling guard is watching from the platform
But through double glazing doesn't hear us shout

He is breathing in the fresh and sunny air
But we breathe in the stuffy smell of us
Caged in and angry that the train is broken
Might an ice cream on the platform soothe our fuss

Of course we're glad to know our course is plotted
By satellites that pass us in the sky
They already know in London that we're stranded
But for an ice cream on the platform I would die

Main Line Traveller

Auntie Jayne writes

Dear Main Line Traveller

I have every sympathy with you, but at least you were not on the Northern Line in rush hour. Actually you were not being tracked by satellite. A GPS system has been developed by British Rail Business Systems in York but is not yet fully operational. It is currently on trial in Scotland and is working well.

Range Rover Chant

Range Fucking Rover
Range Fucking Rover

Screws the World
Screws the World

Over and over.

(And repeat)

Auntie Jayne (2024) writes:

Yes. In How Bad are Bananas (2020), Mike Berners-Lee gives an estimate of the greenhouse emissions for manufacturing a Range Rover Sport as 25 tonnes of Carbon Dioxide Equivalent. That's certainly in the planet destroying range.

However, it strikes me as odd that you have told me that drivers of Range Rovers are the most likely to to stop their cars and help you up when you fall off your bike.

Hate them or love them?

You must be very conflicted.

Lady Lays

Lady lays lawn laze
Love legs lain laid
Love laze last laid
Lady lays lawn laze

Lady lays lawn laze
Love last love like
Look legs lick live
Lady lays lawn laze

Lady lays lawn laze
Love lays lips live
Lick love last lobe
Lady lays lawn laze

Lady lays lawn laze
Look loin lips live
Laid legs loud lust
Lady lays lawn laze

Lady lays lawn laze
Loud loud loud lays
Loud loud loud lays
Lady lays lawn laze

Lady lays lawn laze
Laze laze laze laze
Laze laze laze laze
Lady lays lawn laze

Poetic Parasites

Us poets we are parasites
Don't let us overhear
We smell your brains
And taste your flesh
And store it up for years and years

Us poets we are parasites
Have few thoughts of our own
You'll recognise a bit of this
We also stole a bit of that
And hope the truth is never known

Maps of thoughtful love

I make each map a work of thoughtful love
A shrunken symbol of reality
My contour lines enticing eyes to flow
Down wooded memories you no longer see

But in this age of digital terrains
My eyes have dimmed and I can't clearly think
I feel they want to vectorize my soul
And print it out in polyvinyl ink

Ageing Cartographer

Auntie Jayne writes:

Dear Cartographer

You are getting just a little paranoid. Your artwork is still the best in the business, showing that those special maps need to be finished with the touch of an artist that cannot be achieved using computers alone.

The silence

The silence I remember best
The sureness filling both our breath
No word or thought - just understood
What we were and what we could

The silence I remember best
A double ring of confidence
A lasting bond until your death
Of middle minded reticence

Night worker at Drax - An Obituary

Every day 30 thousand tons of coal
Crushed to dust in a deafening rumble
By speeding cannon balls grinding themselves slowly
Into cast iron cricket balls in a never ending spin cycle

He somehow felt existence in his mind
But knew his thoughts were mere electric flows
As soul and mind were always intertwined
His own electric flows made up his soul

Coal dust blown into the screaming flame
Kept alight for many years on end
As the night lights of the quiet streets of Mexborough
Turn on, turn off, turn on, turn off, turn on, turn off

Sitting at his console every night
Gigawatts of power in his control
He knew his revelation must be right
Electric flows can carry human souls

The heat to boil 50 million kettles in an hour
Forcing steam heated to dryness at 200 atmospheres
Past giant turbines sent to power
Mexborough's lights turn on and off and on and off

Quietly reading by her bedside light
His much loved widow scans and scans her page
Her sadness tempered by a warming glow
Sensing presence from his lingering soul

And outside Mexborough's silent traffic lights,

...turn on, turn off, turn on, turn off, turn on.

He knew his place

Paul knew his social scales by heart
He wasn't a trainspotter he simply liked to
                              travel by train

OK, he did slip the odd engine number
Surreptitiously into his personal digital assistant
Downloading it every night into his laptop

He made sure nobody found his secret out
Especially mother

He knew she would sneer that sneer
She kept for the nouveau Opera Lovers
That bought sets of new CDs from the Sunday
Times

Humans

The Saxons bloody eagled
The Normans drew and quartered

The catholic conquistadors saw
Mrs Clitheroe squashed with doors.

The French Mediterranean slaughter
in the land of a million martyrs.

Auntie Jayne (2024) writes:

Plus ça change.

The conquistadors had nothing to do with the martyrdom of Margaret Clitheroe. That was done by the good protestant burghers of York - because she was a catholic - but I understand your sentiment,

Indeed, the Catholic, <u>The York Oratory recently reported</u>:

"This year we were honoured by the participation of the Right Honourable the Lord Mayor of York, Councillor Margaret Wells, and by the Sheriff, Councillor Fiona Fitzpatrick.

"This was particularly significant, given the Sheriff's role in St Margaret's execution in 1586."

At the Co-op Party Christmas dinner

Dennis (a bit aggressively):

>Was it an all woman short list?

Me (trying to hide embarrassment):

>I don't know how you got a safe seat in the North of England without an Oxford degree.

Unexpected response:

>I've got one.

Me (a bit shocked):

>PPE?

Response:

>Yes.

Auntie Jayne (2024) writes:

>Before Harold Best became MP in 1997, he told me the Labour Party should have a working class section (like it had a women's section).

>However, he said, he'd be the only member in Headingley.

Note for Colin & Gillian:

In this context, PPE means Philosophy, Politics & Economics, Oxford's most prestigious degree in conventional wisdom.

One Ice Cream

I got off the bus near the station.
And bought an ice in Copenhagen.

One ice-cream in Copenhagen buys
        two ice-creams in Stonegate Walk.
One ice-cream in Stonegate Walk buys
        three ice-creams in Budapest.
One ice-cream in Budapest buys
        three ice-creams in Petersburg.

In Mogadishu it is hot.
They don't eat anything a lot.

In Stonegate Walk I sip my tea
With currant buns in autumn sun
Languishing I hear the feet
Sound gently up from Stonegate Street

But Sarajevo's getting cold
Bad for the young
Bad for the old
Bad for the ones that we can see
Nightly dying on our TV

One life's worth in Stonegate Walk is
        fifty lives in Sarajevo.
One life's worth in Stonegate Walk is
        a thousand lives in Mogadishu.

As the storms that ply the atmosphere
Move pressure lows around the world

> The lows of life in Sarajevo
> May swirl around our continent.
> Our continent once so content
> Is showing signs of Mogadishu.
>
> But still it's here I sip my tea
> The autumn sunshine drifting down
> Through roof-lights sheltering Stonegate Walk
> Good for the old. Good for the young.
> The price of life is not in our talk
> Life's price is high in Stonegate Walk.
> In Mogadishu it is low.
> But from the south the winds will blow.

Auntie Jayne (2023) writes:

> That was 1992.

Auntie Jayne (2023) also writes:

> Have you seen TraumaZone by the BBC's Adam Curtis about the failure of the Soviet Union and the subsequent failure of the democracy experiment in Russia. For those of you that refuse to pay a TV licence to the BBC, much of it is available on Youtube .
>
> It makes your poem seem very lightweight

On PoliticsJoe, Adam Curtis said

> What Russia was like 30 years ago - the Soviet Union then - was completely different from

us but its collapse opened the door to the chaos we now have everywhere.

But it was different and one of the reasons I made these films is because I don't think that we in the West understand or fully comprehend what millions of Russians went through at that point 30 years ago.

What happened to them was that their whole world collapsed around them. What they experienced was the collapse of an empire.

The British Empire collapsed - it took 80 years. Theirs collapsed in just a few months and then they were promised a new world: democratic capitalism. Within 8 years that had collapsed in total corruption.

Their whole institutions had fallen apart. People were living in forests, underground and nobody could buy any food -most people couldn't buy any food & the system was being looted by a small number of very rich people.

I don't think we understood what that did to millions of people.

An article Russian Privatization and Corporate Governance: What Went Wrong? by academics from Stanford, Harvard and Maryland Universities, tells how advice from economists from the West helped the failure of Russia's experiment in "democracy".

The authors say:

> In Russia and elsewhere, proponents of rapid, mass privatization of state owned enterprises (ourselves among them) hoped that the profit incentives unleashed by privatization would soon revive faltering, centrally planned economies. The revival didn't happen ...
>
> First, rapid mass privatization is likely to lead to massive self dealing by managers and controlling shareholders ...
>
> Russia accelerated the self dealing process by selling control of its largest enterprises cheaply to crooks, who transferred their skimming talents to the enterprises they acquired, and used their wealth to further corrupt the government and block reforms that might constrain their actions.

Welcome, economists, to the real world of crooks with skimming talents and governments that are influenced by wealth.

Net zero 2030

A tiresome burden our burghers must meekly bear
Is sitting to hear this nonsense once a year
The lie we know is clearly all such rot
Our mayor is forced to say "forget it not"

The cadence of her voice tells us the score
She hates this awful lie she must repeat
But lies like this don't give us any hope
As we heed the awful warning from the Pope

Auntie Jane (2024) writes:

Dear Geoffrey,

Usually poems written to carry political messages are terrible. You may have avoided the worst here - but only just. As you have left it to me to explain the context I will be invoicing you for this extra work.

In 2019, York councillors voted for declaring a climate emergency. In doing so they agreed to "commit to a target of making York carbon neutral by 2030".

At a full Council meeting on 17th July 2024, the Lord Mayor was obliged (by a previous council motion) to remind the meeting of that "York's target for net-zero is 2030".

As you pointed out in a "citizens' speak" slot afterwards the Council's planning rules demanding that many new homes have two car parking spaces, makes net zero impossible for the foreseeable future.

You say that getting to net-zero means no driving, no flying and no consumption of beef, lamb and dairy. That's impossible by 2030. You have a good case for claiming that as York's aim is disingenuous or to put it more directly - a lie.

Pope Francis has said
    "<u>Climate change is the road to death</u>"

OK Paul. One for you.

I will go and lounge on that warm couch under the stairs

    ... in that corner with those old men.

No more fighting the dying of the light.

I'll dream of Python's cartoon boot squashing the World

    ... like a dying fly on the pavement
    ... to quickly end its misery

Then I hope to switch off in a warm comfortable sleep

Before the horrors get worse.

Annie

The Waves of the Dee are soundless.
The seagulls are screechless.
She smells wet estuary mud.
She sees smoke and steam
                from the Llandudno train.
But the seagulls are screechless.

Two wars later I came.
To eat her date, parsnip and banana essence
                sandwiches by the Medway.
On a country road she could feel buses coming
                with her feet.

Same genes, same form, but alien.
A heroine to her alien friends.
(And to me.)

Yesterday surrounded by aliens I remembered
The sound of moving limbs,
The shouted conversations in silence.

She was born when aliens were taught as aliens.
(But, in Ramsgate, at least, with some dignity.)
Before they tried to suppress the signs
like the English suppressed Welsh.

If you dim bastards patronise my clever Auntie again
I'll fucking kill you.

Epilogue

Auntie Jayne (2024) writes:

OK Geoffrey, now you have reached 80, perhaps we could allow you to tell us a few of your 'achievements'.

In the context of this book stick to those that might have political or moral impact but it's a fantasy of yours that your views will be taken more seriously because you are now 80.

Geoff Beacon remembers:

Job Creation

In the late 1960s, I made a (fully costed, revenue neutral) proposal to create jobs without inflation. It suggested raising the nominal rate of VAT but giving employers a rebate for every person they employed. It would subsidise goods that use lots of labour and tax those that don't making it cheaper to employ lower paid workers and at the same time raising their pay.

Because of savings on the dole, the total tax taken would be reduced.

Employing high paid labour and use of capital would become more expensive so their income wold be squeezed.

It could still work.
See A macroprudential proposal for employment.

Planning for car free

Since the mid 1960s I have campaigned against the rise of the motor car which has taken over the space outside peoples homes, where people used to meet and children play. On moving to York in late 1970. I put together evidence against York Council's proposal for an Inner Ring Road, an urban motorway surrounding York City Centre. The Inspector of the public inquiry said that my evidence ("drastic traffic suppression") was the only workable alternative..

See In 1972 I stopped the York Inner Ring Road. Secretary of State, Anthony Crossland cancelled the scheme.

Many of my proposals have since been implemented

The Pollution Tax Association

In 1992, with some neighbours, I founded ThePollution Tax Association. We pay a subscription, which were related to our estimated carbon emissions. Proceeds have gone to green causes or charities.

Conferences on Jobs and the Environment

In the 1990s, I ran conferences for the Co-op Party and Fabian Society, typically on the theme of "Jobs and the environment" and started my first website faxfn.org in order to support a "jobs"conference at the time of the European

Finance Ministers meeting in York in 1997.

York Investigates on York TV

For two years in the early 2000s, I presented my own show on York TV, "York Investigates".

The Green Ration Book

In 2004, I started The Green Ration Book website with a grant from UnLimited, "The Millennium Charity". With the help of friends and neighbours, I formed the Fishergate Environmental Panel.

We made judgements on every day goods and services to asses their carbon footprints based on available research.

Now, Professor Mike Berners-Lee' book "How Bad are Bananas" may be a better source.

However, the idea of having a panel to make judgements still has merit as there are many sources that don't agree and judgement must be used to choose the best ones.

No Miles High Club
In 2008, I started the No Miles High Club. The Press reported "Climate change campaigners from York are setting up a club for people who vow not to travel by aeroplane for a year."

The No Miles High Club was not particularly successful. Flight Free UK have done a much better job,

Yorkmix

I have been a regular contributor to York's local news website Yorkmix.com.

Recent blogging

In 2010, I started the blog brusselsblog.co.uk to share with my friend Robert, who lives in Brussels. In 2015, I started dontlooknow.org. I can't remember why but there's lot's of posts on both websites.

Other

I've been attending various meetings and conferences for several decades and have met and corresponded with many important players in politics, climate and planning policy, particularly through the All Party Parliamentary Climate Change Group when it was run by the excellent Colin Challen, MP. It was a great shame when the parliamentary seat which should have been his was given to yet another PPE.

Colin's book Too Little, Too Late: The Politics of Climate Change can be ordered through Amazon.

Do look up FaxFn, BrusselsBlog and DontLookNow, my main three websites.

Extra: Links to old websites

Here are links to the content of several websites I created.
They were sub-sites of faxfn.org:

- ajoke.universitiesandinnovation.org.uk
- www.planningforterrorism.org.uk
- www.guardianreadersrobthepoor.org.uk
- www.actionagainsttranquillisers.org.uk
- www.arestudentsmiddleclasswankers.org.uk
- www.greeningthegreenbelt.org.uk
- www.plannersattheodpm.org.uk
- www.donttrustyourgp.org.uk
- www.mediastudiesstrikesback.org.uk
- www.theuniversityofplumbing.org.uk
- www.smugbastardsatthebeeb.org.uk
- yorkplotlandsassociation.uk
- £20khousing - a lifestyle revolution

Note on finding references in the text

For those wishing to follow up the links to references in the the text of these poems, copies of the poems that contain links will be found on brusselsblog.co.uk and dontlooknow.org.

Suggested searches:
foreboding site:brusselsblog.co.uk
foreboding site:dontlooknow.org